Advocacy

A review

The Joseph Rowntree Foundation has supported this project as part of its programme of research and innovative development projects, which it hopes will be of value to policy makers and practitioners. The facts presented and the views expressed in this report, however, are those of the author and not necessarily those of the Foundation.

Advocacy
A review

Dorothy Atkinson

Pavilion
PUBLISHING

JR
JOSEPH
ROWNTREE
FOUNDATION

RESEARCH *INTO* PRACTICE

RESEARCH *INTO* PRACTICE

Advocacy

A review

Dorothy Atkinson

Published for the Joseph Rowntree Foundation by:

Pavilion Publishing (Brighton) Ltd.
8 St George's Place
Brighton, East Sussex BN1 4GB

Telephone: 01273 623222

Fax: 01273 625526

Email: pavpub@pavilion.co.uk

Website: www.pavpub.com

The Joseph Rowntree Foundation
The Homestead
40 Water End, York YO3 6LP

Telephone: 01904 629241

Fax: 01222 560668

First published 1999. Reprinted 2000.

ISBN 1 84196 003 9

A Catalogue record for this book is available from the British Library.

Editor: Jeannie Labno

Design and typesetting: Stanford Douglas

Cover photo: Format Photographers

Printing: Paterson Printing (Tunbridge Wells)

Contents

Acknowledgements

There are a lot of thanks to give in a project like this, where so many people have given their time, shared their ideas and told us all about advocacy – as it is, and as it could be. The first person to thank is Lydia Chant, my project co-worker, who has helped plan, design and undertake the project. Her ideas and enthusiasm have contributed to every stage of the project. Also close to home, the advisory panel of Open University colleagues – Sheila Peace, Jill Reynolds, Stan Tucker and Jan Walmsley – has supported us at every stage of the project from outline proposal to final report, Their help in the design and drafting of the report has been especially welcomed. Thanks to Christine Finch, as project secretary, for her overall support of the project, and for her skills in producing clear and nicely laid out drafts of the report. Many thanks to Linda Ward, of the Joseph Rowntree Foundation, for her help and encouragement throughout, but especially for her detailed comments on the report in draft.

In the consultation stage of the project we were in touch with various people and organisations through correspondence, questionnaires, telephone interviews and face-to-face meetings. The views we heard, and the feedback we received, on advocacy in all its diversity and complexity, have contributed greatly to this report. In this context we would like to thank the following organisations and agencies for taking part in the review: Advocacy Partners, Surrey; Association for Residential Care (ARC); Association for Spina Bifida and Hydrocephalus (ASBAH); Aylesbury Vale Advocates, Buckinghamshire; British Institute of Learning Disabilities; Bromley Advocacy Project; Bromley Health Authority; Comic Relief; CAIT (Citizen Advocacy Information and Training); ENABLE, Scotland; Gateway/Mencap; GLAD (Greater London Association of Disabled People); Help the Aged, London; Highland Community Care Forum, Inverness; MACA (Mental After Care Association); Milton Keynes Council of Voluntary Organisations; Mind; MINDLINK, London; Norah Fry Research Centre, Bristol; Northamptonshire African-Caribbean Health and Social Care Resource Centre; NCH Action for Children; National Children's Bureau; NSPCC; National Deaf Children's Association; Oxted CAB Advocacy Project; Quality Assurance Unit (Children's Rights), Dundee; Race Equality Unit; Royal National Institute for the Blind; Sense; Save the Children; Sainsbury Centre; Values into Action; Who Cares? Trust.

Special thanks are due to the people and organisations we visited as part of our review. This was where we came closest to what advocacy means in practice to all those involved. Our warmest thanks go to all the people we met and talked to at the following projects:

- Age Concern Advocacy Project, Nottingham (City Hospital)
- Age Concern Advocacy Project, Walsall
- Allies Advocacy Service, Oxfordshire Mental Health Resource Centre
- Elfrida Society, Access to Health Project (health advocacy for people with learning difficulties), Islington, London
- Granby Community Mental Health Group (advocacy project), Liverpool
- National Youth Advocacy Service (NYAS)
- POhWER, Hertfordshire
- Surrey Advocacy Council, and affiliated advocacy projects
- Voice for the Child in Care (VCC)
- Westminster Advocacy Service for Senior Residents (WASSR).

Chapter One
Introduction

Context

Advocacy at its simplest means 'speaking up' – on one's own behalf, or on behalf of others. In recent years, it has become an important means by which people's voices have been heard, and their views and wishes made known to others. Advocacy operates in many ways. Wherever possible it involves self-advocacy, or self-representation, but often it involves volunteers, practitioners and paid independent specialists being advocates on behalf of others.

Advocacy covers virtually every aspect of human life. It involves support for individuals in everyday living, as well as for people facing a major transition. It involves collective or peer support and action through groups in residential homes, day centres and elsewhere. But it also provides the means by which disabled people, people with learning disabilities, mental health survivors, children, young people and older people, are consulted about services. Advocacy can be an empowering process; it can enable people to gain access to information, to be well informed about their rights, and to make complaints where necessary.

It can do all of these things where it exists, and where it works well. Advocacy, in practice, is piecemeal and patchy rather than universal. This report provides an overview of how, and where, it operates best, and how its potential can be better harnessed through changes in policy and practice. Advocacy has already been subject to considerable research and review. However, reviews to date have tended to be in relation to particular groups of users and/or in relation to specific sorts of advocacy. This report looks at advocacy in the round, in its many and various manifestations.

Aims

The overall purpose of the review was to look at advocacy across the board and across all user groups. In particular, the review aimed to:

- explore recent and current developments

- identify good practices

- clarify strengths and weaknesses

- locate gaps in provision

- draw out key themes and issues

- suggest changes in policy and practice.

Methods

The review was intended to take an overview of advocacy. To get such an overview required a three-pronged approach: a review of the literature; consultation with key people and organisations; and project visits.

The literature review included relevant books, journal articles, JRF publications, Open University course materials, and reports on advocacy commissioned by organisations such as Age Concern.

The consultation phase of the advocacy review involved three stages:

- a review of the in-house literature produced by advocacy projects in the form of brochures, leaflets, annual reports, guidelines, codes of practice and evaluation reports

- a mini-survey of a range of health and social care agencies involved in advocacy, using a short ten-point questionnaire

- telephone interviews with academics, researchers and others with an overview of advocacy.

The final stage of the review involved visits to ten projects. The projects were as wide-ranging as possible, given our time constraints. We aimed to cover projects from all user groups and involving self-advocates, as well as citizen/volunteer advocates, peer advocates and paid advocates. We also aimed to meet and talk to co-ordinators, advocates and, where possible, users of advocacy.

Advocacy, when seen from so many perspectives, is necessarily diverse and complex. Nevertheless, there are things in common between different forms of advocacy, which are highlighted in the report and which serve to underpin and strengthen a movement that is both fragile, yet strangely enduring. And there are differences too: in history, values and approaches. The differences are not always helpful, especially in an increasingly competitive climate where resources are ever more scarce. But differences can also inform – this review looks at the lessons for policy and practice that come out of these differences.

Summary of the report

Advocacy means 'speaking up' for oneself or others. It takes several forms, including self, citizen and peer advocacy, and their many variants. Advocacy matters to people across the whole health and social care spectrum. Where it works well, advocacy is about:

- empowerment

- autonomy

- citizenship

- inclusion.

It involves people working together in partnership or groups.

Advocacy may be long-term or short-term, expressive or instrumental, 'soft' (befriending) or 'hard' (defending) – or any combination of these factors.

Advocates may be paid or unpaid. They may be professional people, trained volunteers or 'insiders' (peer advocates with personal experience).

Advocacy projects have to be approachable, acceptable and accessible to all, but they need to make special efforts to involve people from minority ethnic groups. Advocacy projects are often on short-term funding, and are financially insecure – projects come and go. Some, however, are enduring, but they may have to compromise their independence in order to obtain secure funding.

Advocacy works best where the project establishes:

- a trained and supported advocacy workforce

- aware and sensitive advocates

- good advocacy relationships

- an advocacy culture.

Advocacy is hampered by:

- competing and, sometimes, conflicting interests

- lack of a policy framework

- lack of national standards, training opportunities and guidelines for good practice

- personal and organisational barriers, and institutional resistance

- reliance on short-term funding

- lack of co-ordination and sharing of best practice within and between agencies.

Advocacy has the potential to change things for the better. In order to fulfil its potential, the context in which advocacy operates has to change too. To be effective, advocacy needs money, training, guidelines and credibility.

Advocacy may already be branching out into new roles: as a localised social work service, and as a means of protecting children and adults in residential care from abuse. It is early days yet – more work is needed on exploring these emerging trends.

Chapter Two
Themes from the literature

Advocacy, in its various manifestations, is a relatively recent phenomenon in the health and social welfare field. It grew up in the context of – and in opposition to – the oppression of disadvantaged children and adults, especially those using health and social care services. Its central thesis is that people's views matter, and their voices should be heard. Advocacy is about representation: the representation of one's self and one's own interests, or the representation of the interests of others. Self-representation is the aim and purpose of self-advocacy schemes, groups and organisations.

The wider form of advocacy, the representation of others (including pleading their cause, acting on their behalf and supporting them [Wertheimer, 1993]), takes a multiplicity of forms. It embraces everything from legal, professional and public advocacy, to the widespread use of citizen advocacy in numerous schemes and projects. Self, citizen and peer projects and schemes have proliferated in recent years in relation to people with learning disabilities, disabled people, children and young people, mental health survivors, and older people. This proliferation has been fuelled, in part, by the requirements of the *1989 Children Act* and the *1990 NHS and Community Care Act*. Not only is advocacy seen to be 'a good thing' in its own right, as a means of enabling people's voices to be heard, it becomes more of a necessity where legislation assumes the involvement of the users of services in their design and delivery. This requires at least some attempt at consultation and partnership by service providers, and some means of empowering people – including those people otherwise disempowered and disenfranchised in residential homes and elsewhere – to speak up about their wishes and views. In practice, however, there are many barriers to effective involvement, not least those created by the services undertaking the consultation (Lindow & Morris, 1995).

The two Acts also require that those who provide services ensure that they have accessible and transparent complaints procedures in place. Again, advocacy has a role in ensuring that information is made accessible and that service users are 'empowered', and supported, to make complaints.

Types of advocacy

Advocacy takes many forms but is essentially about speaking up – wherever possible for oneself (self-advocacy), but sometimes with others (group or collective advocacy) and, where necessary, through others. Speaking up 'through others' can involve another 'insider' (a peer advocate), an 'ordinary' person or volunteer (a citizen advocate), or a person trained and paid as an advocate (a paid advocate). All these types of advocacy are important in the health and social care fields. They co-exist but there are fundamental differences between them. The most influential form of advocacy in terms of size, numbers and publications, is citizen advocacy, but its roots in the philosophy of normalisation leaves it open to challenge, particularly by user-led groups and organisations. We return to this point later.

Advocacy can be seen on a continuum: from the 'hard end' of mediation and trouble-shooting to the 'soft end', where the emphasis is more on being a friend, and being there (Webb & Holly, 1993). Put another way, advocacy serves many functions including meeting emotional, as well as instrumental, needs (Simons, 1993). Even where the presenting problem is at the hard end, the closeness of contact can still lead to feelings of friendship and trust. In other words, advocacy relationships are not at a fixed point on a continuum but, like other relationships, they change and grow.

The representation of one's own wishes and needs is a fundamental aspect of human life – and yet it is denied to many people. **Self-advocacy** – speaking up for oneself – is, or should be, the ultimate goal of all other forms of advocacy. It is the starting point here. Self-advocacy has enabled people with learning difficulties to speak out; to have a voice, and to have the means by which that voice may be heard. Self-advocacy has also proved empowering to mental health survivors, and a means of raising the awareness of disabled people about disablist language and images, and discrimination (Dowson, 1991; Brandon, 1994; Brandon *et al.*, 1995).

Self-advocacy has been variously seen as part of the struggle of disadvantaged people for equality, equal rights and citizenship (Williams & Shoultz, 1982), and as a means of altering the balance of power between the person with learning disabilities and other people, particularly those who are close to them, such as parents and staff (Cooper & Hersov, 1986). The self-advocacy organisation, People First, London, says that self-advocacy means 'speaking for yourself', 'standing up for your rights', 'making choices', 'being independent' and 'taking responsibility for

yourself' (People First, 1993). Self-advocacy is seen to have benefits for individuals, as it enables people to have a voice; it enhances personal identity, raises self-esteem and, ultimately, is thought to be empowering (Wertheimer, 1990; Simons, 1992 and 1993; Sutcliffe & Simons, 1993; Mitchell, 1997). Collectively, self-advocacy has become a social movement, which has enabled people with learning disabilities, and people with mental health problems, to influence policy and practice. For example, Survivors Speak Out, a network of mental health system survivors, has harnessed collective self-advocacy – groups of survivors – to work together to press for better services by means of user involvement in their design and delivery (Brandon *et al.*, 1995).

Citizen advocacy is typically seen as a one-to-one relationship between a volunteer spokesperson and their disadvantaged partner. The advocate offers 'emotional support through friendship, spokespersonship, opportunities to learn new skills and help in obtaining needed services' (Sang & O'Brien, 1984). The advocate represents the interests of their partner 'as if they were their own' (Ivers, 1990). A more inclusive view of citizen advocacy is taken by Simons (1993), who sees it as enabling people to speak for themselves wherever possible, and to be their own advocate rather than – or as well as – being a means of representing those who cannot speak for themselves.

Citizen advocacy has high ideals. It aims to empower those who are powerless; to support people who are devalued or discriminated against; and to include those who are excluded – or are at risk of exclusion – from everyday life (Lee-Foster & Moorhead, 1996). Citizen advocacy is based on one-to-one partnerships between unpaid 'ordinary' people and their 'partners'. Citizen advocacy, according to John O'Brien (1987), is:

'A valued citizen who is unpaid and independent of human services creates a relationship with a person who is at risk of social exclusion and chooses one or several ways to understand, respond and represent that person's interests as if they were their own, thus bringing their partner's gifts and concerns into the circles of ordinary community life.'

Citizen advocacy, in its pure form, is independent of services but is interdependent in terms of people; it is a reciprocal relationship, based on the 'act of giving' (Rochdale CAPE project) and the 'gift relationship' (Ivers, 1998). Its reliance on the 'valued citizen' though is problematic in some circles, especially disabled people and mental health survivors. The notion of the 'valued' citizen carries with it the notion of the 'devalued partner'. This is contested as colluding with the 'handicappist structures of society' and as 'able bodied imperialism' (Christie, 1993, cited in Brandon *et al.*, 1995, p98). It puts people into inappropriate, and opposing, social roles and in so doing denies the potential of disabled people, and others, to occupy those 'valued' roles as uniquely experienced and empathetic advocates in their own right. This alternative approach is known as peer advocacy, and we return to it below.

On the other hand, citizen advocacy has proved valuable in the lives of many people with learning difficulties and older people, including some older people with dementia. The organisation Sense introduced a citizen advocacy scheme for deaf/blind and multiply disabled people (Lee-Foster & Moorhead, 1996). This scheme challenged previous conceptions of the limitation of advocacy. It demonstrated that advocacy need not be confined to people able to express their wishes and needs through speech or signs but could be opened up to everyone, including deaf/blind people. The independent

evaluation of the project showed how it had proved possible to recruit people as advocates who could be sensitive to the abilities of their partner – and willing to learn how best to communicate with them. The advocates also brought contact with the wider world; opportunities for visits, outings and friendships; and their own interest and commitment – in circumstances where people had few or no other contacts (Harding, 1995).

Citizen advocacy can lead to friendship, and to an extension of the person's social network. An interesting off-shoot of citizen advocacy is the development of Circles of Support. Rather than a one-to-one partnership, the idea of a circle of support is that it harnesses the interest, and energy, of a group of people. The circle is built up from the inside, starting with people who know the person well, and who in turn are known, liked and trusted by the person. The circle is meant to be long-term, so it offers continuity, even if individuals come and go from within it. Circles are used in relation to disabled children and adults, and people with learning disabilities. For example, CLASP (Community Living and Support Programme) is cited by McIntosh and Whittaker (1998) as offering circles of support to people with learning disabilities. Circles support people through transitions, assessments and reviews. They bring the dual advantages of extending the person's network and lessening their reliance on one person for long-term support.

Peer advocacy also involves partnership, but on a very different basis from citizen advocacy. The advocate in this instance is an insider, someone who is in the know through personal experience of disability or mental health problems, and who can draw on that experience to show empathy and understanding. Peer advocates may be acceptable where other people are not, especially in relation to survivors of the mental health system and disabled people. Peer advocacy is linked with peer support. Mentoring is also very common in the mental health field, where the mentor acts as a role model, coach and confidante – and does so on the basis of personal experience (Brandon *et al.*, 1995).

Independent-living advocates, and peer advocates in Centres for Independent/ Integrated Living, have proved popular and beneficial to disabled people, according to Kestenbaum (1996). Other examples include the Spinal Injuries Association's 'link scheme', which puts members in touch so they can share information and experience; Advocacy in Action, a self-help and workers' co-operative for people with learning disabilities (Brandon *et al.*, 1995); and the Deaf Citizenship Partnership project, which aimed to recruit deaf people as advocates for other deaf people (Reid, 1994). In Manchester, an advocacy scheme run by the Greater Manchester Coalition of Disabled People (GMCDP) recruited disabled people as advocates for young disabled people living in residential homes. The aim was to provide positive role models to support young disabled people in gaining more control of their lives (Greene, 1998).

Children's advocacy in its broadest sense includes volunteers appointed as independent visitors. The job of the independent visitor is to visit a child or young person who is being looked after by a local authority, and who has little or no contact with his or her parents. This is a legal duty under the *1989 Children Act* but one more honoured in the breach than the observance, especially with regard to disabled children and young people. Although independent visitors advocate on behalf of children, they are not themselves advocates. The more usual form of children's advocacy involves the work of paid professional advocates, who represent the wishes of individual children and young people throughout the child-care system but primarily work with those who are being looked after by local authorities.

Independent visitors are volunteers but are recruited, assessed, trained and approved by, or on behalf of, the local authority. Their duty is 'visiting, advising and befriending the child' (*Children Act, Schedule 2, Section 17, (2)*). The independent visitor may be involved as a kind of advocate by listening to, and advising, the child; attending review meetings; and supporting the child in claiming their rights and making decisions (Knight, 1998). Adult volunteers can also become mentors, especially when it comes to giving young people a helping hand when they are leaving the care system. The National Children's Bureau, in association with the Prince's Trust, is running a series of mentoring schemes to help care leavers. Mentoring is also based on a one-to-one relationship between an adult volunteer and young person.

Paid professional advocacy is becoming increasingly important in the lives of children and young people, especially those being looked after by local authorities. It is different in origin and outlook from other forms of advocacy, and involves properly managed and supervised systems for recruitment, training, support and monitoring of advocates. Children's advocacy does, however, share the central principle of citizen advocacy, whereby the advocate represents the child's wishes and views, as the child sees and expresses them. It is seen, and experienced (as this report later confirms) as an enabling and empowering process, built on trust and respect.

The main report covers self, citizen, peer and children's advocacy in detail. There are several other variants to, and derivatives of, these basic models. They will be mentioned in brief here, in order to complete an overview of the types of advocacy currently in use in the health and social care fields, but not all of them will be developed in the main body of the report.

Some advocacy projects and groups have appeared in recent years in relation to 'single issues', such as the sexual abuse of people with learning disabilities, and for adult survivors of child abuse (Malone *et al.*, 1996). In the learning disability field, there are women's groups, for example, the women's health group in Bristol (Clark *et al.*, 1998) and also groups for black people, campaigning groups and independent self-advocacy projects (Sutcliffe & Simons, 1993). In the mental health field, there has been an important 'unprecedented growth' in the 1990s of local service users' forums, patients' councils, one-to-one advocacy schemes and national networks (Read & Wallcraft, 1994). Advocacy, in its various diverse and multiple forms, is a means of challenging an oppressive system and countering the pervasive 'clientism' of services; it is a means to greater empowerment (Stevenson & Parsloe, 1993). Not surprisingly, then, advocacy schemes have proliferated across the health and social care spectrum, and now include crisis advocacy, complaints advocacy, care management advocacy and supported housing tenants' advocacy.

On the whole, advocacy exists alongside but separate from services. Could it be otherwise? Can advocacy be part of the role of practitioners? This is a disputed area, although professionals, such as nurses and social workers, have long claimed to have an advocacy role; saying in effect that they represent and speak on behalf of the people they work with. This claim has been challenged on the grounds that professionals are bound to have a conflict of interests, not least because they are also 'agents of social control' (Brandon, 1991).

Similarly, the development of advocacy within services, through day-centre committees and residents' groups, for example, has also been questioned. Dowson (1991) has criticised the use of advocacy as a 'feel good' idea and concept; in the hands of service providers, he argues, advocacy becomes no more than

a 'fashion accessory', and is trivialised in the process. Similarly, Brandon (1988) has claimed that advocacy is merely the 'velvet glove' that disguises the 'handcuffs' of an oppressive system. Advocacy, it is argued, works best when it is outside and independent of professionals and services; for only then can there be no conflict of interests.

Paid, professional advocacy in the form of service brokerage, provides a means of avoiding a conflict of interests. The service broker is an independent person accountable only to the disabled person who seeks their help. The role of the broker (Simons, 1995a, p65) is to:

> '*Help the person decide what support they need, then (subject to the approval of their clients) design and negotiate a package of services from the most appropriate source...*'

A similar idea to the service broker is the independent living advocate at the Spinal Injuries Unit at Stoke Mandeville Hospital. This is a full-time paid post, where the advocate advises and assists people who have had a spinal injury to achieve their self-defined aims. This has included help with a range of personal and practical problems to do with benefits, housing and relationships, for example, but has also involved supporting people to set up their own independent living schemes, either through a 'third party' agency or by using direct payments to hire a personal assistant (Morris, 1993; Simons, 1995a).

History of advocacy

Although advocacy in the sense of speaking for, or representing, oneself or others, has probably always existed in human society, nevertheless as a social movement it has a short history. Self-advocacy, for example, started as a distinctive movement in relation to people with learning difficulties. It evolved in Sweden and then the USA in the late 1960s, and found expression in this country, in a small way at first, through two 'participation' conferences held in the early 1970s by CMH (the Campaign for People with Mental Handicaps: now known as Values Into Action). Conference participants – people with learning difficulties – spoke for themselves in public about their lives and experiences (Hersov, 1996). The process of 'speaking up' continued through, for example, Mencap's participation forum and the City Lit adult education programme (Simons, 1993; Hersov, 1996). The movement really took off in 1984 when People First, London, was formed by people with learning difficulties who had attended a self-advocacy conference in the USA. Many other local and regional groups have been formed subsequently (Simons, 1993).

Advocacy, in the sense of people speaking out against oppression, has a long history in the mental health field. It can be traced back to the *Petition of the Poor Distracted People In the House of Bedlam* in 1620 and, more recently, to the anti-psychiatry movement of the 1970s and early 1980s (Campbell, 1996). Alongside the dissenting voices, the formal advocacy work of Mind in tribunals and courts was the main means of representation for people with mental health problems until self-advocacy took root in the mid-1980s. This is when, at last, the 'survivors' of the system began to find a voice, and self-representation became important.

The organisation Survivors Speak Out was formed at a Mind conference in 1985. The first SSO conference was held in 1987, and it produced a *Charter of Needs and Demands*. The charter claimed: 'Self-advocacy is about power – about people regaining power over their lives' (Brandon *et al.*, 1995, p70). Survivors Speak Out developed rapidly into a network of individual members and affiliated local self-help groups across the country; by 1992 there were over 100 groups operating

across England, Scotland and Wales (Brandon *et al.*, 1995). Meanwhile, the National Advocacy Network emerged from a national mental health user conference in 1990. The name changed to UKAN (United Kingdom Advocacy Network) in 1992, when it became a federation of advocacy groups run by people who use, or have used, mental health services. Its work involves developing self-advocacy in groups, as well as supporting peer advocacy projects for individuals.

The origins of citizen advocacy have been traced to the USA in the 1960s (Lee-Foster and Moorhead, 1996; Wertheimer, 1998), but it really took hold in the UK in 1981 with the formation of the Advocacy Alliance. This was an alliance of five major voluntary agencies: Mind, Mencap, One-to-One, the Spastics Society and the Leonard Cheshire Foundation. It was launched as a pilot project to introduce citizen advocacy into three long-stay mental handicap hospitals in the London area (St Ebba's, Epsom; Normansfield, Teddington; and St Lawrence's, Caterham).

The model of citizen advocacy introduced by the Advocacy Alliance drew heavily on the ideas of Wolf Wolfensberger (1977) and, later, of John O'Brien (1987). In 1987, the Advocacy Alliance developed into two organisations: the Citizen Advocacy Alliance, which was to continue the work already started in the three hospitals; and National Citizen Advocacy, later to be known as CAIT (Citizen Advocacy Information and Training), an umbrella organisation, which acts as a resource and advice centre to assist the development of new projects. In 1996, the Citizen Advocacy Alliance became Advocacy Partners, an advocacy project that operates in south-east London and Surrey.

The idea of citizen advocacy spread to other user groups. During the 1980s, there was a steady growth in citizen advocacy for older people. Organisations such as Age Concern, the Volunteer Centre and the Beth

Johnson Foundation became involved in setting up citizen advocacy schemes for older people. By 1997 there were around 200 citizen advocacy projects in the UK (Wertheimer, 1998). Projects diversified as they multiplied and, from its origins in relation to people with learning difficulties and older people, citizen advocacy now operates in relation to people with mental health problems, deaf and deaf/blind people.

The history of advocacy in relation to disabled people is more to do with self-help, combined with self, and peer, representation than it is about citizen advocacy. The roots of self-help and self-organisation can be traced, according to Barnes (1998), to the formation in the 1890s of the British Deaf Association and the National League of the Blind. More recently, the development of the independent living movement in the USA in the 1970s proved influential in developing similar ideas in the UK. Thus, a comparable British independent living movement grew up, which pressed for legislation to support independent representation for disabled people. In 1981, the British Council of Organisations of Disabled People (BCODP) was formed as a national forum for developing relevant ideas and action (Brandon *et al.*, 1995).

Subsequently, there has been a proliferation of self-help groups and user-led organisations, such as the Spinal Injuries Association and the Derbyshire Coalition of Disabled People. Self-help, self and collective awareness, and self-representation have been important in the development, in recent years, of Centres for Integrated Living and other user-led and centred services, including advocacy schemes run by disabled people. Citizen advocacy, in its pure form, is eschewed, but in the form of peer advocacy, it is acceptable – as it is in relation to survivors of the mental health system.

Children and young people are in a different position, and the history of children's advocacy reflects this difference. It has an even more recent history. The vulnerability of children, especially those looked after by local authorities, is now recognised (Utting, 1997). This was not always the case and it is only recently that children and young people have been thought to need an independent voice. The need for children to have a voice, and for that voice to be heard, was recognised in the *1989 Children Act*, and by the United Nations Convention on the *Rights of the Child* (ratified by the UK government in 1991). The 'best interests' of the child had long been represented by guardians *ad litem** (and still are) but the child or young person's own wishes and needs were not truly represented until the appointment of advocates for children began in the early 1990s.

Advocacy for children and young people started with the appointment by local authorities of children's rights officers; the first one was actually appointed in 1987 by Leicestershire Social Services Department, although the organisation of Children's Rights Officers and Advocates (CROA) was not formed until 1992 (CROA, 1998).

Parallel movements have also helped the spread of advocacy for children and young people. Important in spreading the reach of advocacy have been the advocacy schemes developed and run by voluntary organisations, such as NCH Action for Children, the Children's Society and the NSPCC; and the appointment of advocates by independent organisations, such as the Voice for the Child in Care (VCC), founded in 1991, and the National Youth Advocacy Service (NYAS), founded in 1998 (and incorporating the two former bodies, Advocacy Services for Children and Independent Representation for Children in Need: ASC and IRCHIN).

---

* A guardian *ad litem*, also known as the child's 'next friend', is appointed under S.41 of the *1989 Children Act* to 'safeguard the interests of the child'.

Principles and values

The principles and values of advocacy have been stated and restated many times (see, for example, Age Concern 1989; Simons, 1993; Wertheimer, 1993, 1998; Dunning, 1995; Williams, 1998). In essence, whatever the type of advocacy, the claims for it remain the same:

- **empowerment:** gaining or regaining the power to take decisions and make choices in all areas of life, large and small (Lee-Foster & Moorhead, 1996)

- **autonomy:** to be a self-determining person; to be seen as unique, and 'to be who they want to be and do the things they want to do' (Stainton, 1997)

- **citizenship:** to safeguard rights; to support the person in being a fully fledged and respected citizen; and to counter injustice (Bateman, 1995)

- **inclusion:** involving and welcoming people into groups and communities, on the basis of equality of opportunity and access (Lee-Foster & Moorhead, 1996).

As we have seen, at the 'soft' end of advocacy, an advocate can be a friend, albeit a special sort of friend. At the 'harder' end, the advocate is an 'unconditional' and 'unambiguous' ally, standing alongside and shoulder to shoulder with their partner; speaking out against injustice, discrimination and 'system abuse', as witness, confidante and go-between (Simons, 1993; Booth & Booth, 1998).

Advocacy in context

Advocacy may have its origins in developments in Scandinavia and North America, but it took off in the UK in the 1980s and 1990s in the context of wider policy changes. The *1986 Disabled Persons Act* was meant to give advocacy a boost by specifying the rights of disabled people to appoint an independent representative; to have access to that representative; and for the person to accompany the user in reviews and interviews, as appropriate. Although this part of the legislation has not been implemented, nevertheless the specification of the right, and the need, for advocacy helped establish a framework in which advocacy could become more centre-stage (Simons, 1993). In the Grampian Region in Scotland, for example, the Health Board and Regional Council used the unimplemented Sections 1 and 2 of the *Disabled Persons Act* as the basis of a range of advocacy projects (Sim & Mackay, 1997).

The *1989 Children Act* (and the *Children [Scotland] Act*) provided a framework in which advocacy for children and young people became possible, and where – given time, commitment and resources – it could flourish. The Act lays down regulations to safeguard all children who are spending some or all of their childhood in care, referred to nowadays as 'looked after' children. The Act introduced a system of independent visitors, and established the need to ascertain the 'wishes and feelings' of children and young people. The requirements are meant to apply to all children, including disabled children, and to cover short breaks, or 'respite care', as well as longer periods away from home.

The system, where it has worked, has meant access to independent advocacy for many children and young people. It works imperfectly, however, in relation to disabled children, as Abigail Knight found in her study of independent visitors (1998). Very few disabled children had access to independent visitors, although where they did, they valued them highly. Similarly, Jenny Morris found, in her study of disabled children in short- and long-term care, that the provisions of the *Children Act* were rarely used to ascertain their 'wishes and feelings' (Morris, 1998a). Not only that, but disabled children continued to be looked after in settings away from their families and their non-disabled peers. The research was supported by a 'reference group' of disabled young people who had experienced being away from home as children (Morris, 1998b). One outcome of the research was the strong recommendation made by the reference group that independent advocates be recruited and trained to represent the views of disabled children. This was seen as a means of promoting and protecting the human rights of disabled children and young people.

Children's advocacy in fact works imperfectly throughout the child care system – mostly because it simply is not there for all the children who need it. In order to boost its provision by local authorities, the organisation of Children's Rights Officers and Advocates brought out a book of guidance based on its experience of advocacy over the last 10 years or so (CROA, 1998). The guidance aims to help local authorities set up more schemes (currently only about a quarter of local authorities do so). The services envisaged are intended to be accessible, to involve children and young people, and to be properly resourced and managed (p7).

The collective self-help organisation of children and young people in care (NAYPIC) folded some years ago. Given the current concern regarding the abuse of children looked after by local authorities, the Utting Report recommended that such a body be reconstituted for young people who are, or have been, in care (Utting, 1997). This recommendation was accepted. The charity First Key subsequently received Department of Health funding to set up A National Voice, a user-led organisation, run by and for care leavers to provide collective rather than individual advocacy. In a related move, the Quality Protects initiative, which sets out a series of key national objectives, was launched by the government with a view to improving

the effectiveness of children's social services (DoH, 1998). Although the programme does not specify children's advocacy as a goal, nevertheless advocacy is necessary in its implementation, as mechanisms will be needed for hearing the views of children and young people, particularly those looked after by local authorities.

The *1990 NHS and Community Care Act* was intended to create a new ethos of care in which users of services would have a greater say in what sort of provision they received. In practice, applying the changes to a 'traditional system of human institutions' was bound to throw up barriers to the involvement of users (Lindow & Morris, 1995, p48). The need to overcome these barriers, and to find ways to consult with and involve users, has led to the growth of advocacy schemes in recent years. Similarly, the need to provide accessible complaints procedures has also boosted the development of advocacy, including complaints advocacy, in order to enable these things to happen (Simons, 1995b; McFadyen, 1997).

Advocacy in action

The 'problem' is that people with learning disabilities, disabled people, older people, mental health survivors, children and young people, are among the least powerful in our society. They may not have a voice nor anyone to speak up on their behalf. A combination of factors, including the disabling barriers of low income, lack of mobility, social exclusion, social prejudice and discrimination, and, in some cases, the 'double discrimination' and simultaneous oppression of being black or Asian and disabled (Baxter *et al.*, 1990), may lead to marginalisation and isolation.

Where social isolation is combined with enforced dependency on carers and others, then people are vulnerable to exclusion, loss of rights and even abuse (Stainton, 1997). This is where advocacy comes in: it claims to take the side of the oppressed and to give a voice to the powerless. Advocacy allows the person behind the label to be seen, and to see themselves, as distinctive – with a history, gender, culture, class and race (Lee-Foster & Moorhead, 1996). Advocacy aims to reduce isolation through having a presence – an advocate who can 'be there', alongside the person, to support them in representing their views and wishes.

Having 'prominent adults as allies' has proved a potent force for some children and young people (CROA, 1998) but this is often not the case for disabled children and young people, as Morris (1998a) reported:

'Most people want someone to talk to them and to take an interest in them, but some of the young disabled people we visited felt that for them this didn't often happen.'

The young disabled people in Jenny Morris's study were isolated through loss of home and family, through having too few friends, and through lack of black, Asian or disabled role models. Their isolation left them vulnerable, and they needed someone to communicate with, to be there, to take an interest, and to work alongside them. Similarly, the young disabled people living in residential homes in Manchester, who were latterly supported by disabled advocates, had hitherto 'been invisible' within the system, feeling abandoned and isolated, and lacking the usual support networks of family, friends, youth workers and the like (Greene, 1998).

Other studies have concluded that advocacy is important in reducing isolation, for example, Lee-Foster and Moorhead's study of advocacy and its impact on deaf/blind people, with multiple impairments (1996) and Tim Stainton's account of how advocacy can reduce the isolation of 'vulnerable adults' (1997). The studies by Morris, and by Lee-Foster and Moorhead,

included children and adults who did not use speech or conventional signs to communicate. This applied to those children and young people who had 'significant communication and/or cognitive impairments' (Morris, 1998a) – the very young people who are often left out of research studies because of the challenges they present to researchers. The removal of barriers to communication by 'imaginative researchers' (Ward, 1997), using pictures, signs, interpreters, facilitators, aids, equipment and a known person, has implications for advocacy with people with multiple and sensory impairments, and where similar barriers to communication need to be dismantled.

Advocacy can reduce isolation – where it exists and is accessible. One outcome of Morris's study was to highlight the need for advocacy for disabled young people who were being 'looked after'. This echoed, to some extent, Abigail Knight's research, which underlined the importance of independent visitors for all children but especially disabled children and young people.

Advocacy can work – but there are many barriers to its availability for those who need it. The barriers operate at all levels: from the structural considerations of who finances advocacy projects, and how they maintain their independence; to organisational issues of who 'owns' advocacy and who it's for; to institutional barriers and defences put up by services and personnel under fire; and to individual conflicts of interest, resistance to change and insecurity. There are also all-pervasive barriers to the inclusion of black, Asian and people from other ethnic minority groups as advocates, or as users of advocacy services. Some advocacy projects, as we highlight later in the report, have taken steps to involve people from ethnic minority groups. Alongside these initiatives there are also many local grass roots projects throughout the country, though mainly

Chapter Three
An overview of advocacy

This chapter reports on the consultation stage of the review. 'Consultation' took several forms. It included a review of in-house literature, as well as information from a short questionnaire and from telephone interviews. The three sources of information were in practice interlinked, as project-based literature was often used by our contacts to supplement their questionnaires and telephone interview responses. The process worked both ways, as sometimes we came across the in-house literature first and followed it up with a personal letter or telephone call. We used the same 10 questions in every case; exploring the literature with the same questions in mind as those we addressed more directly to our questionnaire and telephone respondents.

We got a wide range of responses – we were, after all, aiming to cover advocacy in all its manifestations. And yet, it became apparent that responses followed patterns: there were commonalities between projects and a consensus of views on the basics of advocacy. Differences emerged too; not just differences in details, but fundamental differences about who 'owns' advocacy and who it is for. The report will explore these commonalities and differences, and their implications for policy and practice.

The 10 questions we posed were:

1 What is advocacy?
2 Who can benefit from advocacy?
3 In practice, who has access to advocacy?
4 In practice, who doesn't have access to advocacy?
5 What is good or successful advocacy?
6 What makes advocacy work?
7 What stops advocacy from working?
8 What else could be done to make advocacy work?
9 What are the gaps in provision?
10 What else is there to say about advocacy?

A summary of the 'answers' we received, including information gleaned from in-house reports and so on, is set out below.

1. What is advocacy?

This is a deceptively simple question. And yet we had to ask it. Throughout this report – and throughout the project – we have used our working definition of advocacy based on the idea of 'speaking up' for oneself or others. But what do people involved in advocacy think it means? We asked the question of everybody, and studied the in-house literature, to pull out the definitions and descriptions. We found, as Comic Relief's own review of funded 'advocacy' projects concluded, that there are many possible answers to the question, 'What is advocacy?' This view is echoed by POhWER, a user-led advocacy organisation, which suggests that 'advocacy' is not self-explanatory, and 'can mean many different things to different people'. Its essence though is the idea that everyone, sooner or later, needs help in making their voice heard – and that there are people around who are good at providing the time and support to enable this to happen.

Advocacy may be something we all need at some point, but it has a particular resonance for those young people and adults who, for a variety of reasons, are marginalised from society, discriminated against and, often, excluded from everyday life. In those circumstances advocacy is a lifeline. It is a means of accessing basic human rights.

Put simply, 'Advocacy is about speaking up for oneself or on behalf of someone else according to their needs and wishes' (Morgan, undated, p3). At its heart, 'Advocacy is all about having time for someone and being there at the right time' (Guildford Advocacy Information Network, *Good Practice in Advocacy*). It is about relationships built on trust, where people are valued, respected and treated as equal.

As stated earlier, and confirmed in our review of in-house literature, advocacy is about:

- **empowerment** of people, where possible to be their own advocates: 'We aim to empower people to sort out their own problems for themselves, and realise their own potential as citizens with the rights and responsibilities that entails' (New Connections, Mental Health Advocacy Service, Annual Report, 1997/8)

- **autonomy** and self-determination: 'Advocacy enables people to be more in control of their own lives, by having information, support to make their views known and greater involvement in decisions' (Lochaber Advocacy Service, *Final Evaluation Report*, p3)

- **citizenship:** safeguarding rights, and working towards equality for all, 'A way of promoting equality in practice' (Comic Relief, *Report*, p2)

- **inclusion** of otherwise marginalised people: 'Our aim is to provide an inclusive service to people with mental health problems, regardless of their circumstances, background and culture' (New Connections, op.cit).

In addition to reading the literature, we consulted people using questionnaires, telephone interviews and visits. We asked the same 10 questions of everyone, and received wide-ranging views and comments. The box below (and those that follow) contains a selection of people's direct replies to our questions. The speakers are all closely connected with advocacy – as providers of advocacy, as advocates themselves or as people with an overview of advocacy.

> **The people we consulted told us that advocacy is:**
>
> *'A way of speaking up with or on behalf of another, it's based on a long-term commitment, a trusting relationship, and being there for the person.'*
>
> *'A process by which an individual, or a group, is helped to express themselves; it is particularly important for children and young people who are in care, or are moving within, or leaving, full-time care; advocacy is standing alongside a child so that their "voices" are heard – not always in speech, as advocacy includes babies, young children, and other children without speech.'*
>
> *'A way to defend the interests of a person, and to make sure their needs are met, especially someone who already feels disempowered.'*

2. Who can benefit from advocacy?

The traditional users of health and social care services are the most clearly identifiable beneficiaries of targeted advocacy projects. These may be set up to support self-advocacy or, as is more common, collective self-advocacy in groups. The Highland Community Care Forum in Scotland, for example, was set up in 1993, and now supports a number of such collective self-advocacy projects, covering the spectrum of 'user groups':

- Highland Users Group (mental health)

- Skye and Lochalsh Users Group (mental health)

- Craig Dunain Patients' Council

- People First (learning disability)

- Disability Alliance in the Scottish Highlands (cross disability group)

- Lochaber Action on Disability

- Highland Senior Citizens Network.

(Morgan, undated, p9)

The Advocacy Council in Surrey was launched in 1998: to act as a training and support agency; to develop guidelines for good practice; to raise awareness of advocacy; and to develop an 'advocacy culture' in Surrey (Advocacy Council leaflet). The Council oversees and supports a number of advocacy groups and projects in Surrey, mostly citizen advocacy projects for people with learning difficulties, older people, people with mental health problems and people with physical or sensory impairments. The projects include:

- East Surrey Advocacy

- Age Concern, Surrey

- NSF (National Schizophrenia Fellowship) Advocacy Service

- Elmbridge Advocacy Link

- Advocacy Partners

- Oxted CAB (Citizens Advice Bureau) Advocacy Project.

Although mostly providing citizen advocacy, Advocacy Partners also provides crisis and complaints advocacy:

'Crisis advocacy means listening, providing information and speaking up for others at a time when important decisions have to be made. Complaints advocacy is helping to put things right when they have already gone wrong.'

(Advocacy Partners leaflet, *Crisis and Complaints Service*)

Citizen advocacy is the most widespread type of advocacy. Many in-house documents attempt to define what it is, particularly when trying to engage members of the public in becoming volunteer advocates. The Advocacy Partners information pack, for example, provides a definition of citizen advocacy:

'Citizen advocacy is a means to promote, protect and defend the welfare and interests of, and justice for, persons who are oppressed and who would otherwise be unable to make their views heard, or who are seriously physically or socially isolated...'

The pack also says who advocates are and what they do. Advocates are volunteers who are selected, trained and supported, and who are independent of the agencies providing services. Their tasks are to:

- work with partners on a one-to-one basis

- represent their partner's interests as if they were their own

- foster respect for the rights and dignity of their partners.

(Advocacy Partners information pack)

This form of representational advocacy is important in the children's area, especially children who are looked after in foster homes and in residential care, but also those who make contact for help via ChildLine and other freephone children's helplines. Advocacy is not universal, but advocacy schemes and projects for children are developing all the time. Examples of advocacy providers include the regional and national work of VCC (the Voice for the Child in Care) and NYAS (National Youth Advocacy Service); local projects run by NCH Action for Children and the Children's Society; and local authority appointed children's rights officers and advocates.

Peer advocacy, where the advocate is another 'insider' or user with personal experience or knowledge, has found resonance particularly in relation to people with mental health problems and people from minority ethnic groups. Peer advocacy has also been used in relation to disadvantaged health and social care users who are lesbian or gay; the organisation PACE (Project for Advice, Counselling and Education), for example, recruits lesbian and gay advocacy workers (who may also be service users). The African-Caribbean Resource Centre in Northampton uses advocacy to promote the interests, views and aspirations of African-Caribbean people, especially those who are isolated, lonely and experiencing mental distress.

A variation on the idea of peer advocacy is parent advocacy. The National Deaf Children's Society, for example, supports a peer advocacy scheme run by and for parents. The scheme trains and supports a network of volunteer advocates, most of whom are parents, known as 'local representatives'. The local representatives support families in their area by providing them with information, advice and support. The belief that parents of deaf children can help other parents make informed choices on behalf of their own children has proved well founded. The scheme helps empower parents through promoting access to 'clear, balanced and unbiased information' (McDowall, 1998, personal communication). (See also Barenok & Wieck [1998] for details of the 'partnership policy' schemes, which help parents of disabled

children and self-advocates learn how to be effective in pressing for policy and service changes.)

Although advocacy is far from universal in provision, it has principles that have universal application. Advocacy covers many diverse areas of life. Examples abound, ranging from the provision of generic advocacy services for all-comers (POhWER's 'new directions' scheme); to health advocacy for people with learning difficulties (Elfrida Society, Islington), community health advocacy in Walsall, and continuing care advocacy in Bromley; to advocacy in Rampton and Ashworth special hospitals (in Rampton, for example, the project is managed by MACA, a mental health charity, and recruits advocates for black people, gay men and lesbians, and people with learning difficulties).

> **The people we consulted told us who they thought could benefit from advocacy:**
>
> *'We all can. We all need someone to support us and defend our position.'*
>
> *'Anyone who has difficulty being assertive, or has difficulty with communication.'*
>
> *'Everyone, especially those who are relatively powerless, for example, disabled people, older people, children, people in institutional care (including children's homes and young offenders' institutions), children in foster care, and all children and young people away from home; also children in school, all children using public services, and any child who is isolated and powerless.'*
>
> *'People can benefit from advocacy in different ways:*
>
> - *those being advocated for (if it's good)*

- *those who are advocates can benefit too*

- *those who are listening at higher levels, as it improves their listening skills and awareness*

- *other young people where good advocacy leads to changes in policy and practice, and better outcomes for all.'*

3. In practice, who has access to advocacy?

In theory, advocacy exists for children and adults who, for a variety of reasons, are in need of short- or long-term support. That's the theory. And, in practice, there are examples of advocacy projects that – as we have seen – run across the spectrum of health and social care settings, including: advocacy for children in residential homes and foster care; for children living in their own homes but 'at risk' from abuse or family breakdown; and for disabled children, young people and adults, people with mental health problems, older people and people with learning disabilities, at home, in residential care or in institutions (including the secure hospitals).

Advocacy exists, in principle, for all user groups. However, it is far from universal in practice and is simply not there for everyone who needs it. Who has access to advocacy is often decided by a combination of historical, geographical and financial factors, which determines the start-up of a project (and its continuation) in a particular area. The Oxted and District advocacy project in Surrey, for example, was established in 1996 specifically to support residents of the Royal Earlswood Hospital (a long-stay mental handicap hospital) in resettling into the community during its run-down and closure. The hospital closed in 1997, but the project continues to support people with learning disabilities in their new homes in the community.

The question of access starts with the availability of a project in an area, but there is much more to the issue of accessibility than its actual presence. People need to know about it: to know who and what it is for; to know how to get there and what to expect; and to know if it's the right place for them. Rural areas present particular problems in terms of availability of, and access to, advocacy. Schemes may have to be generic and, therefore, not appropriate for all needs. They may have difficulties recruiting and supporting advocates, and may find that demand constantly outstrips supply, as Webb and Holly found in their study of a citizen advocacy project in Ryedale, North Yorkshire (1994). Access to advocacy in a rural area may require home visits but, as the evaluation of the Lochaber Advocacy Service in Scotland found, this is an expensive option in forms of travel costs and time (White & Clark, 1997).

People have access to advocacy, in the first instance, only if they know it's there. And where it is matters too – advocacy services need to be accessible by public transport, to be physically/wheelchair accessible, and contactable by telephone/Minicom. Additional effort has to be made to make advocacy accessible – and acceptable – to children and adults who are, temporarily or permanently, in circumstances where they need help and support. Access to advocacy also means opening up channels of communication where children, or adults, do not communicate by speech or regular signing. This means that advocacy projects have to promote themselves, and let people know who and what they are for; and to find more and better ways of making themselves approachable.

There are several ways in which projects can make themselves more known and accessible. They can, for example:

- provide information, such as newsletters and leaflets to all 'looked after' children in a locality (NCH Action for Children, Coventry), posters in community settings and articles in local newspapers (Advocacy Partners)

- design accessible information, using a variety of media for presentation, and making sure it gets seen by targeting existing networks (Islington Health Advocacy Project)

- promote the awareness, and take-up, of advocacy, through talks, training and visits (Advocacy Partners; NCH Action for Children)

- encourage people to get in touch, for example, by providing freephone helplines for children and young people (ChildLine, VCC, NYAS), by being situated in approachable places, such as a Citizens Advice Bureau (Inverness CAB Service), and by providing a drop-in facility, especially for children and young people, but also for people with mental health problems (NSF Project, Guildford)

- take positive action to encourage black and Asian people and people from other minority ethnic groups to use the service; this means the recruitment of ethnic minority staff and unpaid workers as advocates to reflect the ethnic origins of children and adults who need advocates (NCH Action for Children, VCC and NYAS make this a stated aim of their projects).

The people we consulted told us who they thought, in practice, had access to advocacy:

'It's the luck of the draw. Even if it's there, people often need someone to help them make the first move.'

'It's hit and miss, especially for people in residential homes.'

'Advocacy is only there for a small number of children, a tiny minority: some of the children in contact with social services, and some of those "looked after" in one form or another.'

'It's very ad hoc. It depends on where you live, and what is available locally. This in turn depends on resources, knowledge and motivation.'

'Advocacy is for people "in the know", in the right category, or who can pay for legal representation.'

4. In practice, who doesn't have access to advocacy?

As we have seen, advocacy is far from universal – but even where it exists, it may not be accessible to people who need it most. So who are these people?

They are children and adults who are in circumstances that make them powerless and vulnerable. According to NYAS, there are 'many thousands of children and young people in the UK today who have no-one to listen to them or speak up for them'. NYAS is doing its best, of course, as is VCC and other children's advocacy services, and the local authority appointed children's rights officers. Nevertheless, many children do not have access to advocacy, including:

- children being looked after by local authorities in residential and foster homes (at any one time, there are 50,000 or more children in this situation, many of whom have already suffered some form of harm, and may be currently at risk in their accommodation: the many deficiencies in the child care system have been charted in the Utting Report 1997)

- young people who are leaving care, often with few educational qualifications, and who may face unemployment, poverty and hardship

- disabled children, especially those living away from home on a short- or long-term basis (see reports by Morris [1998a] and Knight [1998])

- children at home who are at risk because of, for example, family breakdown, school exclusion or poverty, neglect or abuse

- children escaping domestic violence or abuse, for example, homeless children and children in women's refuges

- 'children in despair', who are socially isolated and suicidal.

Who are the adults? They include disabled people who experience discrimination on more than one level. This includes disabled women, disabled parents and black disabled people (Care Management Advocacy Project, CMAP, draft report, *Peer Advocacy in Practice*, p2). People from black, Asian and other ethnic minority groups may have difficulty in accessing advocacy projects across the whole range of user groups. This is often because of language differences, lack of information, shortage of black and Asian advocates and 'colour blindness' of schemes.

Equal Voice in Hertfordshire is a project set up 'to develop advocacy for, and with, people from different ethnic communities; to make sure there is a real and powerful black voice in community care; and to fight discrimination in the provision of community services'. Other schemes have recruited black advocacy workers to develop advocacy with black users, for example, the Westminster Mental Health Advocacy Project. The Lambeth Accord, Black Friendly Project, for black people with learning disabilities stresses the importance of positive images and role models, a point well made by Downer and Ferns (1998). Similarly, the Granby Community Advocacy project in Liverpool aims to provide support by black workers in all areas of mental health and social needs within a non-racist environment; to provide training in peer advocacy to black service users; and to promote user participation and involvement in mental health provision.

Although there are many citizen advocacy schemes for older people around the country, access to them, in practice, remains difficult for people living alone in their own homes with restricted mobility, and even more so for people living in residential homes. Not surprisingly, then, there are very few advocacy schemes for people with dementia or Alzheimer's disease. The few projects that do exist include: Dementia Advocacy and Support, run by Age Concern, Camden; Alzheimer's Concern, Ealing; the Dementia Service run by Westminster Advocacy Service for Senior Residents; the Bradford Dementia Group; and Birmingham Citizen Advocacy, which deals mainly with older people who have long-term mental health problems, including dementia. Otherwise most people with any form of dementia – and their families – are denied access to advocacy.

There are few schemes for women in refuges, or for women survivors of domestic abuse. However, the Hammersmith Women's Aid advocacy project was set up in 1998 to recruit women volunteers to work with survivors. Disabled parents, especially parents with learning difficulties, are in special need of advocacy, but are often least likely to get it. A notable exception in this instance was the Parents Together advocacy support project for parents with learning difficulties in Sheffield (see Booth & Booth, 1998).

The people we consulted told us who they thought didn't have access to advocacy:

'People who are isolated, discriminated against and devalued by society are especially in need of advocacy, and are also less likely to have someone in their lives who would naturally offer to take on this role.'

'Most people! People on waiting lists, those turned away by co-ordinators because they don't have suitable volunteers; people from ethnic minority groups, especially black people with severe learning disabilities.'

'Most children have little or no access to advocacy, but especially those with learning or literacy difficulties, who can't write or use the phone, and have little or no speech. Children in foster care, in practice, also don't have access to advocacy. This is because information is sent to them via their foster parents (and may never arrive) and because even when they know about advocacy most children in foster care are afraid to rock the boat and risk losing another home and family.'

'People who are socially isolated, living on a low income or living in institutions.'

5. What is good or successful advocacy?

To be 'good' or 'successful', advocacy has to work at two levels: the emotional and the instrumental. There has to be a 'feel-good' factor, and there has to be a result. Good advocacy needs both. Whilst it's good to be listened to, and treated with respect, it is also

important that life-changing events and decisions are handled in an effective way.

Advocacy, where it works well, is an empowering process as we illustrate below. This applies across its many manifestations, from supportive self-advocacy groups, through peer-advocacy schemes, to citizen advocacy, and advocacy provided by paid sessional or full-time workers. Advocacy is empowering where it enables people to speak for themselves, and allows them to be heard and respected. Such a process of empowerment leads to increased confidence and self-esteem. Ultimately it can lead to the longer term aim of self-advocacy – or self-determination. (Many reports specify these points in relation to their projects. See, for example, the Bromley Advocacy Project for People with Mental Health Difficulties, *Annual Report 1997/98.*)

People who have benefited from good advocacy make similar points. The Bromley Project's annual report, for example, includes a personal account from a mental health user who recalls how she felt when she spoke to an advocate, rather than to someone from the statutory services: 'Thank God – at last I am speaking to people who don't patronise me and who treat me with the respect I deserve.' The VCC report, *How do young people and children get their voices heard?*, quotes young people who make similar points:

'She explained things which I didn't under-stand. Having the advocate at my review meant they [social services] changed their plans completely. She wasn't boring! She was relaxed and more like a friend.'

(16-year-old boy)

'She was really supportive and really nice. She knew why I was frustrated with social services. She wasn't patronising. She'd always be there when I phoned and would come and see me.'

(16-year-old girl)

'Listened and explained for me so that things got sorted. She helped me say what I wanted and what was wrong.'

(14-year-old girl)

'She gave me the option of doing things I wouldn't have known about otherwise, such as how to go about changing my social worker'.

(16-year-old girl)

(VCC Report, p18)

The young people, between them, say quite succinctly what makes for good advocacy. It involves listening, supporting, explaining, being there, being nice, coming when needed and, of course, enabling each person to say 'What I wanted'. And it has a practical outcome – a better review, a change of direction and new options. Good advocacy means good results. In other projects this has meant, for example:

- more control and choice for disabled people in their community care assessments; and ultimately 'more effective services' (Care Management Advocacy Project, *CMAP Report*, p1)

- access to good quality health services, personnel and information by people with learning difficulties (Islington Health Advocacy Project)

- better quality of life for people 'resettled' from hospital to community, through practical help and support, short- and long-term, and crisis advocacy where needed (Advocacy Partners; Bromley Advocacy Project)

- support, advice and advocacy for victims of racism (Support Against Racist Incidents, SARI, based in Bristol).

The people we consulted told us what they thought made for 'good' or 'successful' advocacy:

'Good advocacy is where it's a "natural" part of the partner's life; where the partner's wishes are put forward "naturally", as if there's no intermediary. For this you need an advocate who is self-effacing and has this "naturalness". It's an important factor but one you can't teach.'

'Good advocacy takes place over time. It's a continuing process. It means heading off problems where possible, but mediating and negotiating where necessary. It requires a very sensitive approach; it's better to go softly, softly making small moves and avoiding confrontations.'

'Successful advocacy is where the ambition is achieved. But even where advocacy apparently fails, and wishes are not met, there may be a measure of success in that the person's views have been expressed, and heard.'

'You need clear objectives for good advocacy. The advocate and the child need to agree on the objectives; to agree, and to know what the advocate is trying to do. The child is, of course, central to the process, and the advocate needs to work towards a respectful and trusting relationship, based on honesty. It's also important to value the child, and their childhood.'

6. What makes advocacy work?

There is no single answer to this question. Advocacy works best, it seems, when four complex, and interrelated, strands come together:

- a trained, supported and managed advocacy 'workforce'

- aware, empathetic and ethically sensitive advocates, able to draw on personal experience
- good working advocacy relationships
- an advocacy culture: a context in which advocacy can thrive.

A trained advocacy workforce

Most projects stress the importance of careful selection, initial induction and training, and on-going training events. The details of training programmes vary but typically include:

- what is advocacy?
- principles and values of advocacy
- role of advocacy
- role of advocates
- good communication and listening skills
- disability equality training
- welfare benefits
- the law and relevant legislation
- role of services.

(See, for example, Oxted and District CAB Advocacy Project Guidelines; POhWER Advocacy Training Course follow-up notes; and the UKAN Code of Practice.)

Advocacy can only work where advocates are supported, supervised and monitored. This applies to all advocates, paid or unpaid. Advocacy can be stressful. It can be a moving or challenging experience. It requires that people become self-aware, and develop the capacity to stand back. For this reason, time is nearly always set aside on a regular basis with the project's co-ordinator, or manager, to allow for talking through the work in hand: to off-load, to make sense of and to reflect on the advocacy partnerships. Advocates are encouraged to record their work in summary form as the basis of personal supervision and for monitoring the project. Informal support is important, too, in making advocacy work,

and most projects encourage informal meetings and get-togethers of advocates who otherwise work alone.

Empathy and awareness

Advocacy works when people bring to the relationship empathy, sensitivity, understanding and action. Some people do this naturally. Others are trained and supported to do it. Mind's Guidelines for Advocates, for example, recommend training in self awareness, empathy, and listening/communication skills. Sometimes user-consultants are employed to help advocates develop these attributes (UKAN Code of Practice). And, of course, peer advocacy is all about using personal experience as a means of understanding, mentoring and supporting people. It provides someone with a role model; an insider to work with who has knowledge, information and experience to share. Advocacy works when people know what it feels like to be disadvantaged, powerless and discriminated against. Disabled people, for example, can make good advocates because of their personal experience and understanding of disability as a discrimination issue (CMAP Report).

Good advocacy relationships

Advocacy works only when the relationship itself works. This means spending time together, developing trust, treating each other with respect, being honest, open and committed. It also means developing interpersonal skills; learning to listen to one's partner 'speak' (or sign, or otherwise make their wishes known); attending to what they have to say; restating it to show understanding; discussing the options and the possible consequences of actions, and considering other options; and finding, and passing on, relevant information, contacts and agencies in order to take things further.

An advocacy culture

Advocacy only works in the right context and environment. This may mean developing 'an advocacy culture', where people are made aware of what advocacy is and what it does (Surrey Advocacy Council leaflet). This applies at all levels. It means making care staff and practitioners aware of advocacy; creating a 'healthy dialogue' so that people accept advocacy rather than resist it (UKAN Code of Practice). It applies to the wider community too. Developing an advocacy culture means going public – newspaper articles, local radio, posters in libraries and GP surgeries and so on – so that people become attuned to the need for, and the possibilities of, advocacy in their neck of the woods.

The people we consulted told us what they thought made advocacy work:

'Advocacy works where there's careful preparation of the advocate, including training which builds on their "natural" skills as an ordinary citizen. An advocate also needs lots of support, not only from the co-ordinator but from other advocates meeting informally over coffee or over a drink in the pub.'

'Advocates make it work. But advocates have to be in a position to make it work. This means that an advocate has to understand their role, to see the need for advocacy and to know the strategies most likely to work.'

'Advocates do best when they are trained and supported. But they also need a supportive agency, which is committed to the principles of advocacy, and a climate which recognises and values advocacy.'

'Advocacy works when there are clear objectives, where there is clarity about the role and an acceptance of the role by other agencies. There is still some defensiveness in residential care, for example. People agree with the principles, and with children's rights, but this may change when they face their first, personal challenge. People don't like it when it affects them, disturbs the balance of power or disrupts the routine.'

7. What stops advocacy from working?

Advocacy is not universal – nor can it be, given the three main constraints that currently operate, and which mitigate its effectiveness. These are, in brief: the tension at the heart of advocacy between citizen advocacy and the disability rights perspective; the policy context in which advocacy operates; and the range of internal and external barriers which prevent advocacy from really taking off.

One of the things that stops advocacy from working effectively is the internal division about what it is, who does it and who it is for. This is a disputed area. The citizen advocacy approach is a practical one: to field valued citizens where they are needed in order to defend the rights of devalued people, and to help alleviate the consequences of discrimination and injustice. No one argues with the need to defend the human rights of disadvantaged people, but there is an argument about who does it and why. Some disabled people see citizen advocacy in its pure form as potentially a devaluing process in itself. Although the relationship between advocate and partner is intended to be supportive and empowering, the fact that it is between a 'valued' and a 'devalued' person suggests a fundamental inequality. The language of 'partnership' is itself problematic. Partnership suggests a two-way relationship, but in practice advocacy partnerships may be quite one-sided (Simons, 1993; Walmsley, 1996).

If it is an unequal relationship, so the argument runs, then it may actually reinforce the perceived dependency of disabled people, and may be a disempowering process (Jones, 1995, p58). An unequal relationship may imply to all concerned 'that disabled people can't represent themselves' (Greater London Association of Disabled People, undated). That is clearly not the case. Self-advocacy is of critical importance for many people and, by extension, so is peer advocacy. There is tension in the advocacy movement, sometimes overt conflict, between its two main driving forces. This does not appear to be a creative tension, instead it seems to be a divisive process. Projects are run in parallel, seeking separate funding and separate human resources; creating a competitive rather than a collaborative environment.

This division runs deep as this view from inside the advocacy movement makes clear:

'There are real differences between our movements, and we do well if we can clarify and respect those differences. Many people who have struggled to create citizen advocacy are pained at the separation from the movement of disabled people. Those who have struggled to stay within service systems and change them are pained by the constant critiques of their efforts. Over time we may hope that our sense of what we have in common will seem greater than what divides us. Most great movements that have changed the fortunes of people have had many strands.'

(Tyne, 1994)

A further constraint that stops advocacy working effectively, is the lack of a coherent policy framework. The *1986 Disabled Persons Act* was meant to provide this by ensuring that disabled people had a right to an independent advocate – but this part of the legislation has never been implemented. Although current rhetoric about involvement and empowerment supports the development of local advocacy projects in order to make these processes happen, a legal framework is needed to ensure that people who need an advocate are entitled to have one. Such a move would help support the development of advocacy on a national basis. A national advocacy body would also be needed to help promote advocacy, to support its development, oversee standards and give informed guidance on training, contracting and evaluation. There are currently no national standards or guidelines for advocacy, even though it touches the lives of society's most disadvantaged adults and children, many of whom are living in the most dire of circumstances. The current 'mish mash' of haphazard provision and practice stops advocacy working effectively (Jones, 1995, p61).

There are a number of more local barriers that stop advocacy working. Paramount amongst these is the question of funding. Projects are funded by a range of local and national trusts, charities and other public bodies, but often the funding is short-term. This militates against longer term planning and, so long as funding remains short-term and precarious, leads to insecurity and uncertainty within advocacy projects. This can throw up a number of additional barriers, such as the shortage of 'people resources' (paid and unpaid advocates, and co-ordinators) through poor recruitment and retention, burn-out, and limited support; and the complicated logistics involved in making advocacy accessible and available to people on a low income, with limited mobility, and who rely on public transport, telephone contact or visits to their home (Jones, 1995, p32).

The more precarious the project, the more likely it is to seek stability. One way to achieve stability is through getting some medium and longer term funding for projects. This may come about through contracts and service-level agreements with local services. This could have an added advantage in enabling projects to make contact with those people who are especially frail, vulnerable or otherwise at risk – and who need advocacy. The trouble is, the closeness of the relationship may compromise, if not the reality, then at least the perception that advocacy is separate from and independent of statutory services. Advocacy must be, and must be seen to be, independent of services. Ironically, the more separate and independent it is, the more likely advocates are to encounter resistance from services, and to experience the reality of institutional barriers. This point was raised with us in relation to territorial disputes between advocates and staff/professionals working in hospitals and residential homes.

A further barrier to effectiveness may be due to the relative isolation and lack of co-ordination between advocacy groups and projects carrying out similar functions. Whilst the independence of local offices allows each one to respond to the local context, the problem occurs when things go wrong, or a situation is seemingly insurmountable. This is where sharing of experiences between projects and across geographical and organisational boundaries would really help. Advocates, by the nature of their work, accumulate experience and develop skills. At the moment, there are few means by which this experience can be pooled and shared by others.

The people we consulted told us what they thought stopped advocacy from working:

'Lack of preparation. Lack of continuing support. Short-term involvement.'

'Lack of funding.'

'Hostility from people working in services. They may support advocacy in principle but they don't like it in practice, and may undermine advocacy by holding meetings when they know advocates can't get there.'

'Unskilled advocates who aren't clear about the role and objectives. Lack of training because there is very little available beyond in-house training.'

'Advocates who have their own agenda, and who act on their own prejudices and beliefs.'

8. What else could be done to make advocacy work?

If lack of secure and medium- to long-term funding stops advocacy working, then the converse probably holds true too: that core funding, with no strings attached, from a central, regional or local source, would help make advocacy work – or at least provide the conditions in which it has a chance to flourish. In the review of 62 projects funded by Comic Relief, one of the key messages was the need for secure funding, so that advocacy projects could 'get on with the work' (Jones, 1995, p2). The wish was not solely for stability, but security without the necessity of compromising their independence through service-level agreements and contracts. Alternative funds were often sought on those grounds, not only from Comic Relief, but also from European Funds, the Single Regeneration Budget and the National Lottery Charities Board (Jones, 1995, p2).

Secure funding makes it possible to invest more in the recruitment, training, supervision and support of advocates. It also makes possible – where appropriate – the payment of advocates on a sessional, part-time or salaried basis. The paid advocate has a key role in relation to children and young people: the level of knowledge, skill and expertise to work alongside children, and to represent their wishes, requires that advocates are trained and professional people. This principle of the paid advocate is being adopted by the Care Management Advocacy Project (CMAP), a peer advocacy project based within the West of England Centre for Integrated Living, but with a key difference – advocates in their organisation will be disabled people themselves. The idea is that core paid staff will develop skills and knowledge over time to act as peer advocates for other disabled people. This is thought to be a much more cost-effective option, as reliance on volunteers often means a constant loss and turnover of personnel, and consequently a loss of skills and knowledge to the project. This is one way to make advocacy work better.

Another way to make it work better is to involve users at all levels of a project. The organisations VCC and NYAS, for example, are advised on their policy and practice by groups of young people; these young advisors also get involved in the selection and training of advocates. The organisation POhWER is a user-led organisation in Hertfordshire. The Board of Trustees and the various steering groups are made up primarily of people who might use – or have used – services themselves. This is 'exemplary advocacy' or 'advocacy by example': a message to all that users of services have a key role in ensuring that advocacy works. An empowerment worker is employed in this instance to enable trustees to carry out their role effectively. All potential barriers are smoothed away:

transport is arranged, information is made accessible, a signer is hired when needed and people are well briefed about forthcoming meetings (Herts Management Consultancy Report, 1998, p16).

Advocacy can only work at all insofar as it reaches the people who need it most. And all sorts of people need it ranging from (disabled and non-disabled) children and young people to disabled adults, mental health survivors, people with learning disabilities and older people. And then there are doubly or trebly disadvantaged people, such as those with multiple and profound learning difficulties; black, disabled and older women and men; frail, housebound older people; people with dementia; and disadvantaged young people. Advocacy projects may need to make special efforts to reach people who are not regular service users – to set up an outreach facility to make contact with people 'at the margins'. The Comic Relief review highlights Blackburn CAB's 'Linkline', which uses publicity, presentations, bilingual volunteers, British Sign Language and disability equality training to make contact with the hard-to-reach people in its target population (Jones, 1995, p54).

The people we consulted told us how advocacy could be made to work better:

'Independent and guaranteed funding from the Department of Health via national voluntary organisations.'

'A higher profile, so that people become more aware of advocacy: much more positive publicity though press, radio, TV and newspapers; money to support a really effective forum to promote and educate people on the values and principles of advocacy.'

'Accredited training, national standards and guidance from government on advocacy and what it means.'

> *'Legislation giving people the right to an independent advocate. All children especially should have a legal entitlement to advocacy, to represent their rights and wishes, and to help them make complaints.'*
>
> *'We need a Commissioner for Children's Rights.'*

9. What are the gaps in provision?

Advocacy works and, in some areas, is flourishing. It could, as we have seen, work better – there is no shortage of ideas as to how this could happen. Many schemes are working on making advocacy accessible and acceptable to all who need it. Outreach schemes have been set up in some places to target the people who need it most. In spite of all this, advocacy is far from universal, and there are many gaps in provision. These have been highlighted already throughout this report, and are just summarised here.

Children and young people

- Children and young people at risk of family breakdown, school exclusion, poverty, neglect or abuse.

- All children living away from home, including residential schools, children's homes and foster homes.

- Children and young people using public services of any kind.

- Disabled children, especially those who are living away from home much of the time or 'looked after' by local authorities.

- Black and Asian children and young people, and children from other ethnic minority groups who are disabled, at risk and/or being looked after away from home.

- Young people leaving care, who are at risk of unemployment, poverty and hardship.

- Children and young people who are victims of domestic violence, including those living in refuges, and those who are homeless.

Adults

Advocacy is relevant to all people who are marginalised, discriminated against and excluded from everyday life. This applies to many disabled people, older people, mental health survivors and people with learning difficulties, but applies especially to:

- disabled women, disabled people from minority ethnic groups and disabled parents, all of whom are likely to experience discrimination on more than one level (Care Management Advocacy Project, undated, p2)

- older people isolated and at home and/or with dementia or Alzheimer's disease; older people living in residential and nursing homes, or geriatric wards in hospitals

- mental health survivors from minority ethnic groups; people in hospital; people 'at risk' in the community

- parents with learning difficulties; people with profound and multiple learning difficulties; people in residential homes and hospitals

- asylum seekers and refugees who are at risk of poverty, geographical dispersal and no-choice accommodation (Asylum Rights Campaign)

- victims of racial harassment and attack who are traumatised, isolated and terrified.

10. What else is there to say about advocacy?

Many claims are made for advocacy, and much of the in-house literature reflected this. Advocacy is thought to be good for people. It is said to be an empowering process, and to lead to an array of personal benefits, such as increased confidence and self-esteem. These claims are universal, and many personal accounts are given in the literature to back them up (see, for example, Bromley Advocacy Project, 1998; also, Williams [1998] and Wertheimer [1998]).

In this section, we look beyond the development of individual confidence and self-esteem, to some of the other possibilities which advocacy may bring in its wake:

- **community involvement**
  This applies particularly to people with learning difficulties who are resettled from a long-stay hospital into the community. The Oxted scheme in Surrey, for example, outlines the steps taken to involve people in clubs and activities in their local neighbourhood, including joining the local library and becoming a member of the local pub quiz team.

- **reclaiming history**
  Advocacy has a role in enabling people to reclaim their own history. This may be done through drama, or other ways of enabling people to draw on their own experience. Understanding the past is one step towards planning and having control over the future (Jones, 1995, pp2 and 45; Atkinson [1998]; Browning *et al.* [1998]).

- **giving something back**
  Some people who have benefited from advocacy have wanted to become advocates themselves, or at least to be involved in the recruitment and training of other people as advocates. This wish to 'give something back' was noted in relation to young people by VCC and NYAS, but also in relation to people with learning difficulties involved in the health advocacy project in Islington.

What else is there to say about advocacy? One advocate looked at her own role and what it means to her:

'It's extremely rewarding to be an advocate. I know it's hard and stressful, but it's really enjoyable. I thoroughly enjoy it, it's what I thought social work was going to be like. There is no other space where adults can work with children, and drop their power.'

Chapter Four

Issues in practice

The final stage in the project was to visit a number of advocacy projects, in order to get a sense of what advocacy is, in practice, and how it operates. How are projects funded, run and supported? Who are the advocates, and why do they decide to take on this role? Who are the people who use advocacy services? What do they think of advocacy and the organisation with which they are in contact?

We drew up a visiting list of projects in order to cover as wide a range of user groups as possible, and to include all the various types of advocacy. In all, we visited 10 projects:

1 Age Concern Advocacy Project, Nottingham (City Hospital)

2 Age Concern Advocacy Project, Walsall

3 Allies Advocacy Service, Oxfordshire Mental Health Resource Centre

4 Elfrida Society Access to Health Project (health advocacy for people with learning difficulties), Islington, London

5 Granby Community Mental Health Group, Advocacy Project, Liverpool

6 National Youth Advocacy Service (NYAS)

7 POhWER: a user-led umbrella organisation for a wide range of advocacy projects in Hertfordshire

8 Surrey Advocacy Council, and affiliated advocacy projects

9 Voice for the Child in Care (VCC)

10 Westminster Advocacy Service for Senior Residents (WASSR).

As we wanted to speak to advocates and users of advocacy, as well as co-ordinators, we prepared a set of leaflets for distribution in advance of our visits. The leaflets summarised the answers we had received at that point to our 10 questions. These were our preliminary findings, taken from our initial literature review and consultation. They were intended to engage people's interest in talking to us, and to provide us with discussion points for our visit, if we needed them. Accessible, easy-to-read leaflets were prepared for children, young people and people with learning difficulties. A one-page request for volunteers to speak to us was also included in the advance package.

We also wanted to talk to people running the advocacy projects, including co-ordinators, managers and chief executives, and in some instances, people with a wider remit for promoting and supporting advocacy projects, such as the Assistant Commissioner for Advocacy in Surrey. We prepared a set of questions to go through during our project visits, covering an array of practical issues, such as funding, recruitment, training, support and access. As all advocacy projects have to deal with these practicalities, we report briefly on them here first.

Organisational issues

The project visits confirmed the short-term nature of much of the funding, and the consequent precariousness of projects. Senior people in several of the projects spent much of their time fundraising in one form or another. Funds were received from a wide range of sources: from local authorities and health bodies, through a variety of means, including contracts, service-level agreements, grants, joint finance, Mental Illness Specific Grants and resettlement funds; from voluntary organisations and charitable trusts, such as Comic Relief and Age Concern; and from the National Lottery Charities Board, the Department of Health and European funds.

Clearly much energy and ingenuity had gone into the funding of projects, but there was a widespread feeling that those attributes – together with the vast amount of time required to complete complicated funding proposals – would be better spent on promoting advocacy. Not surprisingly, several people suggested fundamental changes to the financing of advocacy projects. In the main, this would mean: money from central government, in the form of direct grants for core funding; via local authorities, through top-slicing; or through specific advocacy grants to local authorities to set up independent advocacy organisations. Such a switch, from predominantly local and short-term funding, to more secure central funds, would no doubt bring many other changes in its train.

Indeed, this switch has already happened, at least in part. Our visits covered the spectrum: from the locally-funded projects that recruited trained and supported local people as unpaid advocates, to the professionally managed and supervised advocacy organisations that recruited qualified and experienced people as paid advocacy workers. The latter arrangement was a requirement in relation to children, although it also applied in relation to user-led advocacy for adults. The distinction between advocacy projects that rely on volunteers and those that rely on paid workers, is an all-pervading one. It makes a difference as to how people are

recruited, trained and supported, and to what steps are taken to make advocacy accessible to people who might need it.

The recruitment of volunteers to act as unpaid advocates follows well-tried methods: from posters and leaflets displayed in libraries, surgeries, health centres, social work offices, law firms and colleges; to networking, word-of-mouth, talks, lectures and presentations; to features in local newspapers, and mentions on local radio and television. Special efforts were made in relation to recruiting people from minority ethnic groups, usually involving targeted networking and following up word-of-mouth contacts. The two projects for older people, in Westminster and Walsall, which we visited, had successfully recruited African-Caribbean and Asian volunteers as advocates. The recruitment of paid workers, full-time, part-time or sessional, involved a more formal process of advertising in the national press and in relevant journals. The recruitment of black and Asian advocates, however, also required targeted advertising and the targeting of relevant community organisations. Targeted networking had worked, for example, in VCC, where the appointment of a first black advocate had, by informal means, led to the appointment of others.

Getting people to apply to become advocates is only the first part of the process. The next stage is usually a combined induction/ selection/training process, where the volunteer undergoes an initial information/ training session (which may be two or three days long), combined with informal observation, the screening of people in or out of the projects, or into a specific sort of advocacy and a formal interviewing process. No police checks are made for people electing to work with adults, but written references are usually required. The appointment of paid advocacy workers to work with children requires police checks, as well as references.

The whole process of recruitment, selection and appointment of children's advocates is rigorous; not only do would-be advocates have to show commitment, be skilled communicators and hold child-centred values, but they have to be knowledgeable about the law and the child care system, and have several years experience as practitioners. Again, an initial induction/training programme helps the screening in and out of people, whilst introducing them to the concept of advocacy, its philosophy, values and application. This initial training may be part of an accreditation process, which leads to being appointed, in the case of NYAS, as a sessional advocate; to join a pool of advocates based regionally and nationally, to be called on as and when needed. The advocates we talked to in NYAS were employed full-time as social workers, but acted as advocates in their spare time; evenings, weekends and holidays. Other NYAS advocates are employed in their 'day jobs' as teachers, youth workers and solicitors.

All the projects we visited stressed the importance of support for advocates. This took many forms. Training was seen as a main source of support, and this applied just as much – if not more – to unpaid advocates, as to paid. In the mental health and the child-care fields, the legislation and its application, were main training issues, but people with other specific interests, for example, the dementia advocates in Westminster, received specific training. In their case, this included how to work imaginatively and flexibly with people with dementia using life-story books, reminiscence, music and art.

Informal support was also encouraged in the projects we visited, often in the form of monthly get-togethers, which gave advocates (paid and unpaid) time to talk and share experiences. And, finally, support took the form of supervision – and, again, this applied across the board, regardless of type of project.

Unpaid advocates were supervised by their advocacy co-ordinator and project worker; paid advocates were supervised by their line manager. Records were kept in all the projects about contact with users, and these records were used as the basis for supervision, and also for project monitoring and evaluation.

The other universal, practical issue that had to be addressed by the projects was the question of access. Children and adults had to know about projects in order to use them. The projects had to publicise their presence and did so in a variety of ways: local information and leaflets in libraries, surgeries and other public places; raising the awareness of health- and social-care practitioners, social workers, day and residential services and specific interest groups, such as a local pensioners' group, through talks, presentations and the media; freephone telephone lines (VCC and NYAS, for example, have freephone lines, and also take referrals from ChildLine); through having a physical presence in the right place – a drop-in centre (as in the Granby mental health project), or routine and regular visits to wards in psychiatric hospitals, where advocates become known and trusted (as in the Nottinghamshire and Oxfordshire projects). Some projects had to make special efforts to be accessible. They were the ones that catered for people with dementia; people with profound and multiple learning difficulties, and/or challenging behaviour; people in acute phases of mental distress; and children and adults from minority ethnic groups.

Policy issues

The projects we visited covered a range of user groups, and many different forms of advocacy. They differed in history, funding, philosophy and practice – and yet, they threw up a set of similar issues to be addressed, and dilemmas to be resolved. How these matters were dealt with again varied between projects. Nevertheless, they are worth exploring here as key areas for future consideration in relation to advocacy. At a policy level, two key developments emerged from our project. They are possible signposts as to the future direction of advocacy, and both merit further study. The two developments are: advocacy emerging as a form of social work: and advocacy's potential as a safeguard against abuse. We look briefly at each in turn.

Advocacy as social work

Social workers are not advocates (although they may have an advocacy role), but are advocates doing social work? The Age Concern advocacy scheme in Guildford, for example, accepts referrals from a wide range of practitioners, including doctors, community nurses, care managers, hospital staff and day-centre managers. Advocates found themselves, in practice, fielding a wide range of problems and becoming involved in multiple and complex activities. They are called on to deal with: financial planning; welfare benefits, including appeals and tribunals; rehousing, resettlement and transitions to sheltered units and residential homes; reviews and case conferences; criminal and civil court proceedings; bereavement, depression, mental health and alcohol problems; and 'long-term general support'. This was not uncommon. Advocates in other projects (for example, the Walsall project) reported a similar array of complex problem-solving activities.

Is advocacy filling a gap left by the statutory social services as they concentrate on community care assessments and bought-in packages of care? The evidence from Guildford, and elsewhere, suggests that this is the case; that advocacy often means more than supporting people to have a say in their lives, it means supporting them in managing their lives. Advocates, in practice, seem to be offering a range of practical and emotional support to the disadvantaged and vulnerable people who come their way. Advocacy as the reinvention of social work – or perhaps the return of social work to its roots in the voluntary and charitable sector – is as yet uncharted territory. Further work is needed to explore this development.

Advocacy as a safeguard against abuse

There has been a proliferation in recent times of reports and inquiries into the abuse of vulnerable children and adults, especially those living in residential care. Abuse is possible where people are isolated from outside contact and support, and where there is no-one on the inside to take an interest in their health and well-being, and to ensure that their wishes and views are known, heard and respected. Links with the wider community are necessary because 'people who are isolated and have no allies are vulnerable' (Simons, 1997, p76). Advocacy has a vital role in these circumstances and can make a real difference.

A salutary example of what can happen to people without allies was provided by the case of the Longcare homes in Buckinghamshire. These were private homes for people with learning difficulties. Several residents were found to have been subjected to abuse over a period of years. They had been isolated from the outside world. One outcome of the subsequent inquiry into the homes (BCC, 1998) was that Buckinghamshire Social Services Department made a commitment to developing advocacy, and self-advocacy, as a means of enabling other people in residential care to have a say in their lives. In these circumstances, advocacy is a lifeline, a two-way link between the resident of the care home and the wider community.

The importance of advocacy for children and young people, including collective peer advocacy is now recognised – if not fully implemented. Special efforts still need to be made, however, for disabled young people in residential homes, who are especially at risk of abuse but who can't walk/run away and can't 'say no' (yet have to let adults touch them). Special efforts were made at the Chailey Heritage centre in Sussex to protect the disabled children and young people who lived there. The safeguards included: a children's charter; good practice guidelines; a young people's group; and an independent advocacy scheme (Marchant, 1998).

The importance of advocacy for adults in residential care, as a means of safeguarding otherwise vulnerable adults from abuse, has still to be fully recognised. More work needs to be done on developing advocacy as a protective – as well as a supportive – device, particularly in relation to people living in residential care. Advocacy has the potential to protect people from abuse. How can that potential be best realised? The children and young people's area, with its system of independent visitors, paid advocates and peer advocacy, has much knowledge, experience and expertise to offer in this context.

Practice issues

At the level of practice, the key issues emerging from our visits concerned, on the one hand, the role and impact of advocacy, including how to have credibility as an advocate. They also, of course, concerned the users of advocacy, including their experience of advocacy and what it has meant to them. We will consider each of these issues in turn.

Having credibility

This was a main talking point in the projects we visited, and opinions varied as to how to have credibility. Some people came to advocacy with a professional qualification and background in an allied area, such as social work. This in itself was not enough to guarantee credibility in the eyes of many people who had already encountered such professionals elsewhere in their lives – and, indeed, could be a contra-indication. Advocates in this position, usually paid workers, needed to prove their credibility to potential users through their personal approach; coming over as warm, trustworthy and understanding. The professional background, combined with an insider's knowledge of the system, could, however, buy credibility in other settings and with other professionals, particularly in relation to formal reviews, appeals and planning meetings. This could stand the young person, or the mental health survivor, in good stead when their 'case' was heard, and their views were represented by an advocate in the know.

Advocates without this kind of background, and without an accredited training in advocacy, could feel disadvantaged – and less than credible – when they had to deal with institutions and the staff and professionals who ran them. Residential and nursing homes, and hospitals in particular, could be hostile environments for advocates. This led to some people feeling that they needed to have a comparable status with the professionals they had to deal with; to be qualified as advocates, through appropriate accredited training. This view was expressed by both paid and unpaid advocates, but it was a minority view. Most people stressed the need to be credible in the eyes of users, and that meant credibility of a very different sort:

- as a 'passionate' defender of the rights of disadvantaged people (the words 'passion' and 'passionate' were used a lot)

- as a role model, for example, several older people became advocates and some joined the management committee of the Westminster Advocacy Service for Senior Residents, thus acting as positive role models for older people using the service; the co-ordinator of the Walsall Elderly Asians project acted as a role model for the elderly women users, who themselves became more confident; and, the autonomous black advocate in the Granby mental health project was a powerful role model for the black users

- as an insider, for example, a dementia advocate in the Westminster project used to manage residential homes herself once, so was able to overcome institutional barriers and staff suspicion

- as a diplomat: paths could be smoothed by tact and diplomacy; the Granby project, for example, felt the credibility of its paid workers was due in part to the time spent by the advocacy manager in working with institutions, agencies and service personnel to pave their way.

Having an impact

We met many advocates, and talked to them about their role and their impact. We include two short accounts to illustrate that advocacy can, and does, make a difference to people's lives.

'Jenny', advocate from VCC

'I enjoy my work. Advocacy is hearing all of it, not just what the child or young person is saying, but what it means, and what's not being said. It means talking through the implications of what they want, so they know.

'Most children in care already have at least a social worker and a carer, but the advocate has a different

relationship; she represents their wishes, not their "interests". Advocacy is not part of the welfare system in which the child or young person has grown up, and on which she or he has become dependent. The advocacy relationship is different because the child chose it, and the child is the driving force. This can be empowering and transforming, as the child begins to see herself as a person.

'Advocacy is a significant role, and one that has status, especially in review meetings. It compares well with the status of carers who are, sadly, seen as very lowly, and are often ignored or talked over. Advocacy can change the dynamics of a meeting, and can swing things in the child's favour. But it doesn't always work and, when it doesn't, you end up sharing the child's powerlessness.

'Advocacy is one means of improving services. Carers, social workers too, are disempowered at grass roots level. The advocate can support the child's wishes and help them take a stand; and can see their point of view instead of labelling them or blaming them, as even social workers are wont to do.'

'Alan', advocate from NYAS

'I'm a social worker and a guardian ad litem, as well as an advocate. Having an advocate can be incredibly important to a young person. Your presence can help a lot in reviews. Sometimes social workers change their mind before a review if they know that an advocate is going to be there.

'With the young person, we spend time together talking through the options and rehearsing different possibilities.

> *The point is, **they're in charge**, I'm not there to talk for them, but to represent their wishes. I promise complete confidentiality unless they're in danger in any way.'*

Involving users

The projects we visited varied in the extent to which they involved users other than as the recipients of the service. Two or three projects simply did that. But others did much more. In fact, we found examples of users involved at all levels of projects, and in all capacities:

- as trustees (on POhWER's Board of Trustees, supported by an Empowerment Worker)

- as a policy officer with an input to policy development and planning at County Hall (this is a person with learning difficulties, with a supporter, representing self-advocacy groups at county level, in the *Speaking Up in County Hall* project, supported by POhWER)

- as advisers, trainers and presenters in an organisation: the Young Persons' Panel in NYAS, for example, takes a hand in policy making, selection of advocates, training programmes and public presentations on the work of the organisation

- as advocates, both paid and unpaid, where inside experience is valued; examples include: older volunteers in Westminster; the mental health survivor volunteers in Oxfordshire; and the users/disabled people who work at all levels in the various POhWER projects.

Telling your story

Stories are told a lot in the advocacy movement. They have been a key feature in the self-advocacy movement, as they are a means by which people with learning difficulties have come to represent themselves, and thereby gain recognition. Some groups represent this in their title: the People's Lives group in Hertfordshire, for example. Stories are also told in relation to citizen advocacy (see, for example, Wertheimer [1998] and Williams [1998]), as stories bring advocacy to life.

Stories were being told – and used as part of advocacy – in two of the projects we visited. A group of young people at VCC have produced a book of stories: *A Shout to be Heard* (VCC, 1998). This had proved an empowering process, and the group had continued to meet as a campaigning and pressure group. More stories are planned, this time using the medium of video.

Stories were also used in the Westminster dementia project. The advocates who worked with older people with dementia spent time getting to know them and building up a relationship. This involved understanding the symbolic language often used. It also meant spending time reminiscing; enabling the person, in whatever way suited them, to talk about their past. Where it worked, this was a way to enable someone to keep hold of what could otherwise be a fragile sense of identity.

Giving something back

Where advocacy works, it is empowering. And when people feel empowered they want to give something back. We found examples of this process in several of the projects we visited. We include spokespersons from two of them.

Voice for the Child in Care

'Justine'

'I've had a long experience of the care system. I've been in children's homes from nine to eighteen, which is what I am now. For two years, I tried to get social services to let me go and live in a foster home of my choice. They didn't do anything. They let me down, so I stayed in the children's home.

'I knew about advocacy because my brother used it. It worked for him too. He was in a children's home with me, but when he got to eighteen, he was kicked out by social services. He had nowhere to go, so the carers let him stay but referred him to VCC. That's how I knew about it. I needed help in using the complaints system. I had an advocate to work with me, on my behalf, so that I could make a proper complaint against social services. It took three years.

'I think advocacy is really important. I had no-one, no family, nowhere to run to. I came here as a refugee, with just my brother and sister. Every child should know about advocacy. It's really important to have someone to talk to, someone who is independent, outside of social services, someone who's there for you.

'I'm part of a group of children who've been in care. We meet once a month, to talk about how we feel, get up-to-date news. We also campaign for more advocacy for children and young people in care. We have been to conferences and meetings, and talked about our experiences. We talked to politicians, including Paul Boeteng. We also talk to advocates, to make them even better than they are – we help with training.

'I'd like to be an advocate in the future. I think I'd have something to offer because I know what it feels like from the inside. I'd use my own experience. I also know what it's about: having a choice, having a say in moving or staying put, and having someone to talk to.'

The Access to Health Project, Islington

This project has empowered people with learning difficulties to use the health service. This is what it set out to do, and it succeeded – but it also empowered people to do more than gain access to health. We met some of the people involved, and heard how advocacy for health was, in fact, a springboard to consultancy work and community-based advocacy.

'Sandra'

'I'm a consultant, mainly for people with learning difficulties. It's to help with training doctors. I show what happens in the surgery, like I'm the patient, and I'm seeing the doctor. Then I'll play the doctor, and show how to get on with your doctor, like if you've got a problem, how you speak to him.

'We're going to a conference, me and Michelle [health advocate], and I'm quite chuffed about that. It's a big conference but we've got two lessons on the Saturday and that's where we do the two interviews. We do the nasty doctor, ask people to do their forms to say what they think, then I bring the nice doctor on. The nasty doctor can't be bothered to talk to us, can't be bothered to listen. He doesn't listen, *doesn't know what to do, he just sits there answering the phone.'*

'Kevin'

'I don't like doctors and nurses, they don't listen. I've had two advocates, one to help with health and one to help me see my children. Advocates are a great idea. Advocacy helps people. If I didn't have an advocate I wouldn't see my children for four hours a week. She's made me speak up more. I won't ever be frightened of social workers again, it's been great. They don't listen. I think the reason they don't listen is because I've got a learning difficulty and if you've got a learning difficulty they don't want to listen.

'I asked my advocate if there was any chance of me being an advocate and she's trying to get someone to train me. I feel it would be a good idea, like I'd give people what they gave me. Having an advocate with a learning difficulty, you don't get that every day. They're trying to get me in at the community advocacy place because they've got nobody there with a learning difficulty who will speak up in the community.'

Chapter Five
Conclusions and implications

Advocacy works. It works across diverse contexts and different cultures, and it takes many forms. Advocacy, at the moment, is a hotch potch of local, regional and national schemes, largely unco-ordinated and unregulated, and often relying on untrained and unpaid volunteers. Schemes, as we have seen, are often funded on a short-term basis. As a result they are precarious, and not all of them survive. In fact, advocacy works in spite of the tensions that beset it, and the practical difficulties caused by muddling through with few resources.

Advocacy works because people make it work. People who are committed to the concept and practice of advocacy, and who feel 'passionately' about its mission, make it work. Is that enough? Can advocacy survive on commitment and passion? Surely it cannot. In the children's area, advocacy is provided by independent and paid workers who are supported, supervised and managed by their employing advocacy organisation (or, in the case, of children's rights officers, by their local authority). This approach works well. A similar approach is used in the user-led organisation POhWER, but on the whole is relatively little used in relation to advocacy for adults.

Is this the way forward? Advocacy is fragile and fragmented. It needs to be coherent and co-ordinated, otherwise there will always be schemes that fold, gaps and shortfalls in provision, and people who happen to be in the wrong place when they most need advocacy.

Advocacy is on the fringe of things. It is time it moved much more centre stage and became a real force for change. It has that potential. But it needs a boost – or several boosts. One possible boost is the recommendation by the Royal Commission on long-term care that the Government starts to give its backing to the development of local advocacy schemes (Royal Commission Report [1999], recommendation 8.12). This Report relates to older people but the principle of the 'independent intermediary' relates equally well to others. This is one boost – another is A National Voice for children and young people. What else could make advocacy a force to be reckoned with? The following suggestions arose directly from our review:

- **a legal right** to advocacy, so that disabled and disadvantaged people have a right of access to an independent advocate

- **a national advocacy network:** mapping and listing of schemes, so that links can be made between them; these links could be strengthened through local, regional and national conferences, seminars and workshops, where ideas and experiences about advocacy could be shared – and which would include schemes for children as well as adults

- **long-term funding**, without strings, to support advocacy for children and adults

- **guidelines** for advocacy organisations, including codes of practice for recruitment, selection, training and supervision (the best and most rigorous practice seems to occur in advocacy schemes for children and young people)

- recognised and accredited **training in advocacy** leading to a qualification (training possibilities for advocates are currently very few)

- **legal status** for advocates; advocates need credibility and status in order to be in a position to represent people's wishes separately from, and independently of, the statutory services (Values Into Action are developing a 'nominee representative' scheme along these lines for people with learning difficulties)

- advocacy projects to be at least user-centred and, where possible, to be user-led; but always to **involve users** at every level of the organisation.

Advocacy could become a force to be reckoned with. But will it? It has the potential, as this report has shown, to become an informal branch of community-based social work. It could also become the best way of safeguarding against abuse, especially in residential homes. How far it goes in either of these two directions remains to be seen.

References

Age Concern (1989) *Guidelines for setting up advocacy schemes.* Mitcham: Age Concern England.

Atkinson, D. (1998) Reclaiming our past: empowerment through oral history and personal stories. In: L. Ward. (Ed.) *Innovations in Advocacy and Empowerment for People with Intellectual Disabilities*, pp115–126. Chorley: Lisieux Hall Publications.

Barenok, T. & Wieck, C. (1998) Partners in policy making: far more than the object of policy. In: L. Ward. (Ed.) *Innovations in Advocacy and Empowerment for People with Intellectual Disabilities*, pp233–243. Chorley: Lisieux Hall Publications.

Barnes, C. (1998) Disability, disabled people, advocacy and counselling. In: Y. J. Craig (Ed.) *Advocacy, Counselling and Mediation in Casework.* London: Jessica Kingsley Publishers.

Bateman, N. (1995) *Advocacy Skills: a Handbook for Human Service Professionals.* Aldershot: Arena.

Baxter, C., Poonia, K., Ward, L. & Nadirshaw, Z. (1990) *Double Discrimination. Issues and Services for People with Learning Difficulties from Black and Minority Ethnic Communities.* London: King's Fund Centre.

Booth, W. & Booth, T. (1998) *Advocacy for Parents with Learning Difficulties.* Brighton/York: Pavilion Publishing/JRF.

Brandon, D. (1988) *Putting People First.* London: Good Impressions.

Brandon, D. (1991) *Innovation without Change? Consumer Power in Psychiatric Services.* London: Macmillan.

Brandon, D. (1994) Peer advocacy. Care in Place. *The International Journal of Networks and Community* **1** (3) 218–224, December.

Brandon, D., Brandon, A. & Brandon, T. (1995) *Advocacy. Power to people with disabilities.* Birmingham: BASW/Venture Press.

Bromley Advocacy Project (1998) *Annual Report and Accounts.* Bromley, Kent.

Browning, R., O'Brien, J. & O'Brien, C. L. (1998) One day at a time: changing a system to realise a dream. In: L. Ward. (Ed.) *Innovations in Advocacy and Empowerment for People with Intellectual Disabilities*, pp23–38. Chorley: Lisieux Hall Publications.

Buckinghamshire County Council (1998) *Report on the Longcare Inquiry.* Buckinghamshire County Council.

Campbell, P. (1996) The history of the user movement in the United Kingdom. In: T. Heller, J. Reynolds, R. Gomm, R. Muston, & S. Pattison (Eds.) *Mental Health Matters: a Reader*, pp218–225. Basingstoke: Macmillan.

Care Management Advocacy Project (CMAP) (undated) *Peer Advocacy in Practice.* Unpublished draft report.

Children's Rights Officers and Advocates (CROA) (1998) *On the Rights Track. Guidance for Local Authorities on Developing Children's Rights and Advocacy Services.* London: Local Government Association.

Christie, J. (1993) Speaking for ourselves. *GLAD* (App III) London: Glad.

Clark, D., Fry, T & Rodgers, J. (1998) Woman to woman: setting up and running a health advocacy group for women. In: L. Ward. (Ed.) *Innovations in Advocacy and Empowerment for People with Intellectual Disabilities*, pp129–140. Chorley: Lisieux Hall Publications.

Cooper, D. & Hersov, J. (1986) *We Can Change the Future: Self-advocacy for People with Learning Difficulties*. London: National Bureau for Handicapped Students.

Department of Health (1998) *Quality Protects*. London: Stationery Office.

Downer, J. & Ferns, P. (1998) Self-advocacy by black people with learning difficulties In: L. Ward. (Ed.) *Innovations in Advocacy and Empowerment for People with Intellectual Disabilities*, pp141–149. Chorley: Lisieux Hall Publications.

Dowson, S. (1991) *Keeping it Safe: Self-advocacy by People with Learning Difficulties and the Professional Response*. London: Values into Action.

Dunning, A. (1995) *Citizen Advocacy with Older People*. London: Centre for Policy on Ageing.

Greene, M. (1998) *Over To Us. A report of an advocacy project working with young disabled people living in residential institutions*. Manchester: Greater Manchester Coalition of Disabled People.

Greater London Association of Disabled People (undated) *Gladpack Handout 1*. London: GLAD.

Harding, T. (1995) *The Sense Advocacy Project. An Evaluation*. London: NISW.

Hersov, J. (1996) The rise of self-advocacy in Great Britain. In: G. Dybwad & H. Bersani Jr. (Eds.) *New Voices, Self-Advocacy by People with Disabilities*. Cambs., Mass.: Brookline Books.

Herts Management Consultancy (1998) *POhWER Review*. Unpublished report.

Ivers, V. (1990) *Policy Document: Advocacy*. Beth Johnson Foundation.

Ivers, V. (1998) Advocacy. In: Y.J. Craig. (Ed.) *Advocacy, Counselling and Mediation in Casework*. London: Jessica Kingsley.

Jones, D. (1995) *Review of 'Advocacy' Work*. A report for Comic Relief.

Kestenbaum, A. (1996) *Independent Living. A Review*. York: JRF.

Knight, A. (1998) *Valued or Forgotten? Independent Visitors and Disabled Young People*. London: National Children's Bureau.

Lee-Foster, A. & Moorhead, D. (1996) *Do the Rights Thing!* An Advocacy Learning Pack. London: Sense.

Lindow, V. & Morris, J. (1995) *Service User Involvement: Synthesis of Findings and Experience in the Field of Community Care*. York: JRF.

Malone, C., Farthing, L. & Marce, L. (1996) *The Memory Bird. Survivors of Sexual Abuse*. London: Virago.

Marchant, R. (1998) Letting it take time: 'rights' work with disabled children and young people. In: L. Ward. (Ed.) *Innovations in Advocacy and Empowerment for People with Intellectual Disabilities*, pp183–198. Chorley: Lisieux Hall Publications.

McFadyen, J. (1997) Mental health advocacy and the path to participation. *British Journal of Health Care Management* **3** (9) 475–482.

McIntosh, B. & Whittaker, A. (1998) *Days of Change. A Practical Guide to Developing Day Opportunities with People with Learning Difficulties*. London: King's Fund.

Mitchell, P. (1997) The impact of self-advocacy on families. *Disability and Society* **12** (1) 43–56.

Morgan, G. (undated) *Proposals for Development of Advocacy in Highland*. Unpublished draft report.

Morris, J. (1993) *The Independent Living Advocate Project: Final Evaluation*. London: Spinal Injuries Association.

Morris, J. (1998a) *Still Missing? The Experiences of Disabled Children and Young People Living Away from their Families*. London: Who Cares? Trust.

Morris, J. (1998b) *Don't Leave Us Out. Involving Disabled Children and Young People with Communication Impairments*. York: JRF.

O'Brien, J. (1987) *Learning from Citizen Advocacy Programmes*. Georgia: Georgia Advocacy Office.

Oxted and District CAB Advocacy Project (undated) *Guidelines for Volunteer Advocates*. Unpublished in-house guidelines.

People First (1993) *Self-advocacy Starter Pack.* London: People First.

POhWER (undated) *Advocacy Training Course: Follow-up Notes.* Unpublished in-house document.

Read, J. & Wallcraft, J. (1994) *Guidelines on Advocacy for Mental Health Workers.* London: Mind/Unison.

Reid, C. (1994) *Deaf Citizens in Partnership.* London: RNID.

Royal Commission on Long Term Care (1999) *With Respect to Old Age: Long-term Care – Rights and Responsibilities* (Sutherland, S.), cm 4192-I. London: Stationery Office.

Sang, B. & O'Brien, J. (1984) *Advocacy: The UK and American Experiences.* London: King Edward's Hospital Fund.

Sim, A.J. & Mackay, R. (1997) Advocacy in the UK. *Practice* **9** (2) 5–12.

Simons, K. (1992) *'Sticking up for yourself.' Self-advocacy and People with Learning Difficulties.* York: JRF.

Simons, K. (1993) *Citizen Advocacy: the Inside View.* Bristol: Norah Fry Research Centre.

Simons, K. (1995a) *My Home, My Life. Innovative Approaches to Housing and Support for People with Learning Difficulties.* London: Values into Action.

Simons, K. (1995b) *I'm Not Complaining But…* Complaints Procedures in Social Services Departments. York: JRF.

Simons, K. (1997) *A Foot in the Door. The Early Years of Supported Living for People with Learning Difficulties in the UK.* Manchester: National Development Team.

Stainton, T. (1997) Can advocacy eliminate abuse? Critical components of an effective advocacy system. In: *Speaking Out Against Abuse in Institutions: Advocating for the Rights of People with Disabilities*, pp93–102. Ontario: Roeher Institute.

Stevenson, O. & Parsloe, P. (1993) *Community Care and Empowerment.* York: JRF.

Sutcliffe, J. & Simons, K. (1993) *Self-advocacy and Adults with Learning Difficulties.* Leicester: NIACE.

Tyne, A. (1994) Taking responsibility and giving power. *Disability and Society* **9** (2) 249–254.

United Kingdom Advocacy Network (UKAN) (1997) *Advocacy – A Code of Practice.* London: NHS Executive.

Utting, W. (1997) *People Like Us. The Report of the Review of the Safeguards for Children Living Away from Home.* London: Stationery Office.

Voice for the Child in Care (1998) *A Shout to be Heard.* London: VCC.

Walmsley, J. (1996) Working together for change (Workbook 3). *K503, Learning Disability: Working as Equal People.* Milton Keynes: Open University.

Ward, L. (1997) *Seen and Heard. Involving Disabled Children and Young People in Research and Development Projects.* York: JRF.

Webb, B. & Holly, L. (1993) *Citizen Advocacy in Practice: the Experience of the Scarborough–Ryedale–Whitby Advocacy Alliance.* London: Tavistock Institute.

Webb, B. & Holly, L. (1994) *Evaluating a Citizen Advocacy Scheme.* Findings, Social Care Research, 52. York: JRF.

Wertheimer, A. (1990) *A Voice of Our Own: Now and in the Future.* London: People First.

Wertheimer, A. (1993) *Speaking Out: Citizen Advocacy and Older People.* London: Centre for Policy on Ageing.

Wertheimer, A. (1998) *Citizen Advocacy. A Powerful Partnership.* London: CAIT.

White, J. & Clark, A. (1997) *Lochaber Advocacy Service, Final Evaluation Report.* Highland Community Care Forum.

Williams, P. (1998) *Standing by Me. Stories of Citizen Advocacy.* London: CAIT.

Williams, P. & Shoultz, B. (1982) *We Can Speak For Ourselves: Self-advocacy by Mentally Handicapped People.* London: Souvenir Press.

Wolfensberger, W. (1977) *A Balanced Multi-component Advocacy Protection Schema.* Toronto: Canadian Association for the Mentally Retarded.